THE SANDSTORMS

Written by

Roger Downton

Traveller's Joy Publishing

Funny, brilliant, hilarious, moving, informative, side-splitting, heartrending, shocking, tragic, warming, pathetic, humiliating, sympathetic, stimulating, amazing, get on with it!

It wasn't until the 70's that any of us realised that the 50's and 60's had happened!

Published by Traveller's Joy Publishing

www.thesandstorms.co.uk

ISBN 0-9550166-3-0

Printed by
Printed by Remous Ltd, Sherborne, Dorset. www.remous.com

Cover photograph (Pavilion Bournemouth)
courtesy of Gerry Atkins (dancer)

OTHER WORKS BY THE AUTHOR

IN WAR HEROES WAKE (book), Traveller's Joy Publishing

PART ONE ORDERS (screen play)

Tony and Yasmin Risotto present The Comedy Magic Instructional Show (DVD), Traveller's Joy Publishing

Corkscrew Play Chuck Berry (CD)

Corkscrew Play American Appalachian Hillbilly – English – Irish – Scottish (CD)

All My Own Work (CD)

SYNOPSIS

This dramatic, nostalgic, informative, hilarious, and sometimes touching story turns the metaphoric spotlight on to the teenage years of a bunch of ambitious, spirited, innocent, optimistic young blokes who, boiling with the irresistible human urge to create, on the verge of their adult lives, and through their own volition, created The Sandstorms rock group. Located in Bournemouth, it could have been any town during hedonistic times.

The big names and famous know who they are, and so do we, and sometimes we hear rather too much about the same people trawled up by the media in interviews, compilations and such programmes. This book, on the other hand, is written by me, Roger Downton (lead guitar), to honour The Sandstorms rock group which incorporated Roger Downton, Dave Hitchings (drums), Tony Haberfield (rhythm), Mike Brown (1st bass), Joss (1st vocalist), Dean Fane (2nd vocalist), Eddie Hodges (2nd bass), Dave Woodbury and John Hutcheson (occasional keyboards) and many other groups that became the backbone of our local music scene in and around Bournemouth during the late fifties and early sixties. On the world stage of entertainment, we ranked as locally known, but we were a life form, we existed, and that fact cannot be eradicated. Remarks such as 'big fish in a small pond' may be used pejoratively, but to those who profess to know it all, I say, the truth is: we were there, we were a working, popular rock group, we lived the dream, we grew up with it, and we have all the amazing memories associated with those heady times, and now we would like to share those dynamic, laughable, sensual, thought provoking, embarrassing, and enlightening of times. Enjoy the trip; learn what and who inspired us. There are some funny and some bumpy bits.

A familiar tale for anyone who ever sorted out the difference between a verse and a chorus, it starts with a dream.

The Sandstorms came out of a particular time and place, but their story could easily have happened since. In love with rock 'n' roll, all they wanted to do was pick up their guitars and play. They did it and in doing so they had the time of their lives.

It doesn't matter if you're baby boomers like them or not, if you've ever been a teenager with a head full of hope and a heart full of song this is your story too.

Nick Churchill, Bournemouth Daily Echo

TOPICS INCLUDED IN THE STORY ARE VERY ABSORBING SUCH AS the acquisition of our **first instruments**, our exposure to all the late 50's/60's **music**, the famous **bands** and artists of the time, and our burning desire to emulate their success and become fabulous rock idols in our own right. **Venues** and **agents** and **girls** and **Big Bands** and **gigs** and **punch ups** and **snogging** and **equipment** and **fans** and **Mods-n-Rockers** and **hair fashions** and **rehearsals** and **sackings** and **transport** and **bubble-n-squeak** and **costumes** and **jobs** and **froffy coffee**, and **food** ..... well, all kinds of thrilling things.

THE AUTHOR OFFERS HIS INESTIMABLE THANKS AND APPRECIATION TO THE FOLLOWING

I could not have written this without the unfaltering editorial skills, companionship and love of my adorable wife Sandra, to whom I am forever deeply indebted.

I also offer my gratitude to Dave Hitchings, co-founder of The Sandstorms rock group. We had some laughs; it was short lived but intense. We were all mates (Tony, Mike, Dean, Eddie, Joss, Dave, Roger, Dave, John), but unknown to us, we were playing a diminutive, but important part in a gargantuan piece of musical history.

I am thoroughly indebted to my parents for their total commitment to my dreams, good or bad. I thank them also for displaying their staunch support, steadfast unfaltering encouragement, resourcefulness, and importantly, financial backing. They endured hundreds of hours of practice noise that went way beyond the call of reasonable parental duties. I know they enjoyed every minute of it.

THE NAMES OF THE PROTAGONISTS are factitious, and I sincerely hope that my portrait of them is flattering, honourable and in no way offensive to their sensibilities, families, associates and friends. With regard to dates, times, names and incidences, and in order to make easy flowing, interesting, light-hearted reading, I have invoked my artistic licence. All topics and stories are based on the truth, but should not be seen as a diary, or definitive record of details, people and events. Just relax and read.

FOREWORD

After being presented with the idea of Roger's book, one thing about his group's experiences in the '60's resonated strongly with me. The Sandstorms were doing the same thing that I and many of my musician friends had done in Phoenix, Arizona, during the mid and late-Fifties.

We banded together in small groups, and played different venues, performing the popular music of our day. The basic difference was that our heroes were Elvis Presley, Bill Haley, Les Paul, and Hank Williams, etc., and we listened to them and played their material at our gigs. Not very many years later, the entire music scene had changed, and The Rolling Stones, Beatles, myself and my contemporaries was the music that The Sandstorms listened to, and played at their gigs. Our job, and the job of all those thousands of local groups in cities throughout the world, was to reproduce the hits as closely as we could, in a live setting for people to dance to or simply sit and enjoy. Many of these groups became quite big stars locally and enjoyed a loyal following of fans.

Most successful artists and musicians who later became well known around the world began their careers in this way, then proceeded to make a full time career of their music, while some musicians decided to be much more sensible and just do it for fun. They realized they needed to seek out a better paying career to support themselves and the young families they were beginning to acquire.

I was one of those who chose to make a career of my music and was lucky enough to discover a successful way to do this. I'm very honored to be thought of as one of the next generation's 'heroes', and to know that I inspired some people to become musicians and play in a rock and roll band.

I want to thank Roger for his very kind words. It gives me a good feeling to be told that I contributed to The Sandstorms and influenced their music back in the early days of Rock and Roll.

Duane Eddy

CONTENTS

NOTES ON THE AUTHOR will put some flesh on the bones, and give the reader and archaeologists of pop some idea of this particular protagonist. Roger Downton is a chap who was a child of the mid forties, and a teenager of the late fifties and early sixties. He was an only child and was nurtured by Charles Percival and Gladys Rose, his loving (not in a slushy way), committed and caring parents. They owned a successful business in the locality of Kinson, Bournemouth, and were well-known and active pillars of the village. Roger enjoyed a Spartan, tough, rugged, outgoing childhood, and was always one to stretch and challenge the boundaries of conformity. He wasn't a gutter snipe, or a revolutionary, but he was inquisitive with a burning zest for life. Until reaching his teens, his mother insisted, and rightly so, that he be attired in short trousers, tweed jacket and a school cap. The reason – because that's what young boys wore. The uniform was renewed on a regular basis, before the new school term, and, frustratingly for Roger, it always had to be one size too large. Reasoning never worked, as the trite man in the shop always insisted, "He'll grow into it." Nevertheless, on becoming a teenager and a rebel with many a cause, Roger began to flex his individuality and dressed for the time. But most importantly, it was a statement reflecting his own idiosyncratic attitude ..... whatever that was? As a semi grownup, anatomically, Roger was of regular construction. Joss, the vocalist, used to call him 'baby face', an irritant for one struggling to be taken seriously as an adult. Height – average (5' 8"), size 8 shoes, and a head that would be comfortable in a 6-n-7/8's hat. Hair followed the rest of the flock, brushed back at the sides, quaffed on the top, and later, as trends dictated, turned somewhat modish.

Roger favoured smart, tight fitting three piece suits made by Austin Reed, the bespoke tailors in Westover Road. Suits usually took up to six weeks to complete, including a couple of fittings, when enthusiastically, the tailor would go to work with a tape measure, disconcertingly running it up the inside leg, whilst coining confusing, timeless phrases such as, "Which side do you dress, sir?" When ordering a suit, requirements on cut-n-design were extremely fastidious, even down to the shade of the buttons, and Roger was a stickler for accuracy-n-detail. For example, the sleeves had to be short enough to reveal the hand-made shirt cuffs and ornate links. Trouser legs were pencilled, and their lengths were to be such as to display a good portion of the trendy platform boots, previously purchased on the King's Road, London. There were many criteria that the conservative, dyed-in-the-wool needle pushers of Austin Reed found rather outlandish, and the arrogant demands of this upstart young whippersnapper chaffed uncomfortably against all their hard learnt craftsmanship and traditional suit making instincts. Roger justified his radical requirements by the fact that a handmade suit cost him £22, and that princely sum amounted to several hard-earned months' wages. There was a lot of attention to detail with regard to dress and hair and girls and cars and guitars and amps. Unfortunately for Roger, he was a born entertainer with a strong comedic bent, something, which to him, has always been an impediment, and caused him much rancour-n-torment. Descriptive, defining words would be, determined, obsessive, single-minded, driven and always focused on presenting the best possible show. He doesn't bare fools gladly, and is concerned about the destruction of the environment by the pure selfish greed of conglomerate elements. A lack of action worries him, particularly by governments who have the real power and their fingers on the buttons that can make things happen, but are all too intimidated by the manipulative barons of business-n-war. Roger also likes to get it off his chest.

In the late fifties and early sixties, Roger was recognised as an accomplished guitarist and fluent trumpet player. Thus, and as a reflection of his outstanding musical skills and entertainment refinements, he was soon engaged by the prestigious Jan Ralfini Orchestra. Later, he served as a Rifleman and section N.C.O. in The Royal Green Jackets. Roger played trumpet with the Bournemouth Silver Band whilst at school, playing at half-time on the pitch at Dean Court Football Ground, and in the bandstand at Fisherman's Walk and Bournemouth Gardens.

He also played the trombone with The Band of The Royal Green Jackets for a brief period of his military service. Seeing service in Germany during the Cold War, and noticing an opportunity to wield his past – dormant – hairdressing skills, Roger, forever enterprising, seized the initiative and ran a small sideline business as the RGJ Regimental barber. Thanks to the kindness of the upper echelons of the Battalion, he was allocated two mornings per week, for two hours, to practice this reasonably lucrative, drinking-money, trade. His main task as a Mechanised Infantry N.C.O. was as a Commander on board a dual personnel (commander-n-driver) Ferret armoured car reconnaissance vehicle, accompanied by his always humorous driver, Ginger. Many hair-raising jaunts across the German landscape, following the East-West border, were taken very seriously in the light of a real threat of nuclear annihilation from, what was then, Communist Russia. Leisure time was occupied playing in a rock and R&B group, he formed, called The Flunky, which appeared at many military and German venues, and received glowing reviews in Deutsch Zeitung. Many of his close friends in the Army were killed. They are remembered with much affection.

Today, at the time of writing, Roger lives with his wife and fellow artiste, explorer, musician and speaker, in Poole, Dorset. He enjoys their well stocked, rambling style garden, growing vegetables for Sandra who is vegetarian, and tending to the grass. Minding the shrubs and eradicating the weeds is a regular feature of life, plus the tri-annual task of replacing the felt roof on the garden shed. He would like to keep chickens-n-pigs, but they are far too demanding and would simply become pets. This latent desire for a menagerie harks back to a blessed childhood when his parents kept pigs, goats, dogs and some geese. His Mother would often be seen sitting alongside the kitchen doorstep, plucking a chicken for their Sunday dinner, or making mouth-watering rock cakes, some of which he would steal as they cooled outside on a wire trivet. Even at the delicate age of six, Roger was acutely aware that hanging for cake theft was no longer tolerated. Like him, his Mother was also aware of that fact, and so occasionally, but most rarely, carried out her own judgement, sentencing and exacting punishment with a very well aimed, stinging slap to the back of the leg. Nothing was wasted in those austere days. All the chicken feathers became stuffing for pillows, and the bones made delicious broth. Schooling was something to be endured, and the last exit from its rusting wrought iron gates of hell was like being released from the confines of a brainwashing institution. All that misery, and lack of academic qualifications, was remedied by the experience and rich diversity that life, in its infinite and perplexing random wisdom, chose to hurl at him. Proverbially, like the ancient practice of mudslinging, some of it stuck.

GO...

It was like a romance. I was smitten and found myself engulfed in a time enduring, uncompromising deep-seated and faithful relationship. The pleasure is always the same, sensual, unselfishly altruistic, passionate, but never disappointing. The only difference from most relationships is that mine is with an inanimate object. I know I'm not alone with this infatuation and millions will empathise. The subject of mon amour ..... guitars. Playing a guitar, even in solitude, can be comforting, relaxing, agreeable company and can afford one a warm glow of satisfaction. Its therapeutic qualities are calming to the mind-n-soul, but on the other hand, it can be stimulating and encourage action and clear thought. Remember the little drummer boy, striding ahead of the massed, red coated ranks of soldiers as they marched into battle. Of course, he would always be the first to be killed, so not such a good gig. Naturally, this can be applied to any choice of instrument, but as a duty of care, I must point out that caution should be observed, and all exposure should be administered in a professionally prescribed manner. If in doubt, or concerned about over dosing, consult a musical wizard.

The Sandstorms rock group played every Tuesday and Saturday for the Beat Nights held in The Pavilion, Bournemouth. Because we were considered good enough by the various managements, agents and bookers, and they felt confident with us as a band, more often than not, we were re-booked and regularly placed alongside many well-known performers. There was, of course, the understandable characteristic, greed. We had a bit of a following and a fan club, so bookers were certain of ticket sales.

The Jan Ralfini Orchestra

I (Roger Downton, lead guitar of The Sandstorms) was also a member of the Jan Ralfini Orchestra, and front man (guitar/vocals) in the resident rock quartet (drums, sax and bass), an offshoot of the Jan Ralfini Orchestra in The Pavilion Ballroom. We were billed as 'Roger and The Rallies' and accompanied all the visiting major artists and bands performing at The Pavilion. The Jan Ralfini Orchestra was the resident Big Band – Joe Loss/Glenn Miller style – at The Pavilion Ballroom. The ensemble comprised of a brass section with trumpets and trombones, tenor and alto saxophonists, a pianist, a percussionist, a bass player, and me on guitar, and we performed nightly for the thousands of serious-n-novice dancers who frequented the dance floor. Jan Ralfini was our middle-aged, immaculately dressed band leader, a maestro who always cut a dash in his tastefully tailored lounge suit, neatly folded bowtie, and squeaky mirror-like patent shoes. Members of the band were uniform in matching red blazers, black trousers, white shirts and smart little black bow ties. All very sober, the exception being on Latin American nights when we all pulled-on our ostentatious, multi-coloured, puffy silk shirts with the big fluffy sleeves. Before we began to play, Jan would walk amongst the band and issue us with a selection of rattles, marimbas, maracas, parrot whistles and all manner of Latin American-style percussive items. This was our rare opportunity to let slip the regular formalities, and behave like a bunch of delinquents. During the up-tempo, hot Latin rhythms, we shouted out things like, "Arreeeba, arreeba," accompanied by screeching, high pitched tongue rattling, brrr-aaa-haaa's.

Every night, with the controlled upright posture of a regimental sergeant major, Jan would stand proudly at the front of the stage, facing the audience, his back to his competent orchestra of professional musicians. Beating the strict ballroom tempo in the air with his demonstrative arms and conductor's baton, he would encourage the dancers with a wide sincere smile. An interesting and outstanding feature of Jan's distinguished appearance was his neatly manicured, thin black, narrow lined moustache. Jan Ralfini was suave beyond compare. Always equally immaculate were the erect, angular, rigidly poised dancers who every evening swirled serenely across the ballroom floor in their glittering sequined gowns and flowing tailed suits. Once a medley of tunes, cha-cha-cha, waltz or foxtrot, was completed, Jan would spin round on his heel to face us in the orchestra, whilst simultaneously announcing, "And the next dance please". With his face to the band, and the warm glowing dancers wandering casually back to their tables for a short, one tune intermission, Jan would produce a white cotton handkerchief from his trouser pocket. Raising it to his lips, he would discreetly, but quite bizarrely, whip out his false teeth and surreptitiously despatch them into his jacket pocket. Minutes later, as we approached the final bars of the interval tune, our toothless conductor would then seamlessly replace his gnashers, and once more, grinning a confident but false, toothy smile, invite the oblivious dancers back onto the floor. There was even more of Jan's duplicity to come. One morning, whilst collecting some music from the Ralfini family flat on Bath Hill, I noticed, as he handed me the manuscripts, and whilst I struggled to engage in some puerile small talk, that to my astonishment, he'd shaved off his moustache! I was quite taken aback because it made him look so bland. His top lip was barren, bereft of life, like the deforestation of a rain forest. Anyway, that same evening, as per normal, Jan arrived on stage, straightened his back, masterfully lifted his chin, raised his baton to strike up the music, and to my disbelief and surprise, the moustache had reappeared! It was back in its usual place, on his top lip, nestling underneath his nose. I couldn't believe it. A pencilled moustache!

It was a great honour for one as young as me to be granted the opportunity of working alongside much older, middle-aged but highly skilled musicians. They all took the rudiments and formalities of music very seriously, and were definitely not prepared for the introduction of rock bands and popular music. In the dressing room, their opinion of all these hairy, Neanderthal, guitar thrashing, upstart pop musicians was quite churlish. "Three chord wonders" was their mantra, and "It won't last, people will soon get fed up with all that racket." 'All My Loving', a Beatles' tune, had just been released, and that came in for some serious disembowelling criticism. "Have you heard the guitar rhythm?" one of the trumpet players sneered. "You can't do that, that's the drummer's rhythm," he pompously concluded. I dared to chirp in with, "I think it's great, creative, brilliant." The tenor sax player, aghast at my young audacity, retorted with the stinging rebuff, "Yes, well, you're a guitarist, and they all have ears like brick walls." I loved my time with them; they were dedicated musicians and they taught me a lot, but it took me decades to realise that I really didn't know all I thought I knew, and now I know that all I know is that life is nothing like I thought it was going to be, but just what it always was, and always will be. Then you expire to a heaven of milk-n-honey, which only makes you sick and rots your teeth.

We were bursting full of alacrity; we were tenacious, dedicated, and enjoyed our fair share of local fame, good-n-bad gigs and groupies, but we were always dreaming that some cigar smoking impresario would discover us and rocket us to a life of dizzy fame, money, parties in country mansions with swimming pools, booze, fast cars, and fast women. Even if those criteria were not quite met, we had a great time, and we are happy to have been an integral link in the spine of popular musical history.

A FEW SALIENT POINTS, a précis, just to give an idea of the particular time in history that we're thinking of: compared to today, things were extremely primitive, that isn't to say that life wasn't worth living, on the contrary, we were industrialised and basically modern, but it was a less technologically reliant society. There were values and discipline, and things were simpler and much more pleasurable. Don't argue with me, I was there!

IN THE BEGINNING there were no CD's, DVD's, Videos, Walkmans, I pods, or electronic tutorials for learning the guitar, apart from Bert Weedon's book, Play-in-a-Day. I'd heard instrumentals, such as 'Peter Gun', 'Shazam' and 'Cannonball', played by that phenomena, and maybe the only other main man, apart from the unsurpassable Chuck Berry, to popularise the guitar ..... "Ladies and Gentlemen, I give you, the one-n-only, Mister ..... Duaaane Eddy." Yes, it was Duane Eddy, the archetypal King of Twang's deep, gutsy sound that made the guitar so attractive to me. His, 'How low can you go?' bass note tone epitomised what the electric guitar should sound like. It was showy, and when, or if, I ever learnt to play, would attract an audience. I pondered over the theory of how he achieved that invigorating 'twangy' sound. Duane Eddy had an obvious impact and moulding effect on our own, home-grown, wonderful Hank Marvin of The Shadows. Listen to 'Apache', and The Beach Boys ('Surfin U.S.A.') who famously borrowed some of their big hit intros from Chuck Berry and Duane. All I knew then was that I needed to be plucking that stuff, and apart from good old Bert and his book, our only other means of acquiring the skills to play the latest tunes was to analyse 45rpm singles and 33rpm LP vinyl records. Skiffle was still popular, and Lonnie Donegan had been to The States, raked over some old folksy Hillbilly music, re-arranged it, and was storming the charts. He also created some memorable homespun, jokey songs, as with 'My Old Man's A Dustman', and 'Does Your Chewing Gum Lose Its Flavour On The Bed Post Over Night?'

Mass death and devastation of the Second World War had blighted the whole world for six years, and had not long finished. There was still rationing, but in spite of it all, over the bomb craters and rubble and ruins of their towns, nations were looking forward to a bright new start. Nazism had been vanquished, and things were going to be different; there was hope pumping through the veins of the new generation. There was a long way to go. At that time, mid fifties, there were no mobile 'phones, internet, computers, fax machines, microwaves or satellite navigation, and the telly (for those who had one) was still mostly in black-n-white. TV for kids was in the format of Children's Hour, and it was just that, an hour, after which you were packed off to bed in a freezing cold bedroom (no central heating), huddled under the sheets, blankets, eiderdown and candlewick bedspread, not forgetting the hot water bottle, to keep warm. Entertainment mostly came via steam radio, e.g. Listen with Mother (are you sitting comfortably?), and Sunday Night at the London Palladium was on the telly. Steptoe & Son was real to us; the rag-n-bone man still came round on a horse-n-cart shouting something incomprehensible ..... "Raaagboowwwneeuuugh!" As a small child, some of my most memorable holidays were spent with close relations in the historic Navy town of Portsmouth. I relished the chance to spend the day sat up on the front seat of a horse-n-cart, the hairy footed shire, slowly clip clopping, plodding through the endless maze of terraced houses, delivering its cargo of fresh vegetables door-to-door. At lunchtime, the horse was given a nose bag and would chomp happily away at the hay inside. Late afternoon, when dusk drew in, the greengrocer would light a hurricane paraffin lamp that was suspended on a long bouncy stick to illuminate our trotting gait back to the mews. Those lost Halcyon days! Many of us long for those simple, un-technical times. Critics (usually those who weren't around) dismiss our pining melancholy as misguided rubbish. Yes, there *were* some nasty bits, there still are, but that's just how life is, get over it! Over all, we were happy, contented, courteous and respectful, a happy breed. "We few, we happy few, we band of brothers and sisters."

YOU MAY WONDER WHY WERE WE CALLED THE SANDSTORMS and I'd like to take you on a fascinating journey, and open a Pandora's Box of mystique, intrigue and revelation, with perhaps a crafty, unexpected twist at the end, like we did last summer, Chubby Checker. Then there was Little Eva with 'Come on baby, do The Loco Motion.' And Bee Bumble and The Stingers, singing 'On Blue Berry Hill'. Sorry, where was I? Oh yea, what was behind the name of The Sandstorms rock group? I'll cut straight to the chariot race, and admit the truth and no longer hold the suspense of which I'm sure you are being held in. Fact is, it's nothing more profound or meaningfully deeper than I really liked the tune, 'Sandstorm'. It was recorded by Johnny and The Hurricanes on a 45 revolutions per minute record, and sat sitting on the reverse side was the curiously titled 'Beatnik Fly' which sounded more than a bit like 'Jimmy Crack Corn'. If I was interested enough to delve deeper, I could probably find a story behind that name. "But quite frankly my dears, I can't be arsed, can you?" On the other foot, if you're anorak enough, do a web search. We played several Johnny and The Hurricanes tunes, 'Jacks Good', 'Trambone' and...and..?

THE SANDSTORMS ROCK GROUP was formed in the late fifties, and played into the early sixties (1964 actually), and great fun it all was too. Believe it or not, there was even a Sandstorms Fan Club, with a proper registration form and few hundred devoted members. It cost two shillings and six pence for one year's membership with an official card issued to each member. A hard core of female fans would always be in attendance at our gigs, sometimes wearing silk sashes across their chests (made by themselves) with the slogan, 'We love the Sandstorms'. From what I remember, in my forever decreasing brain cells, our female fans were equally supportive, forward and just as aggressive as they were with well-known artists. I clearly remember one girl in particular who lay in wait for several days at the entrance of my employment (John Stewart Ladies Hair Stylist)

in Westover Road. Every time I came out, perhaps to deliver some clean towels to our other salon, a couple of shops away, she would follow me along the pavement, demanding that I take her out. Having been politely refused a few times, she then decided to physically and quite energetically attack me. Suddenly, and without warning, taking advantage of my disadvantage – an armful of laundry – she tackled me and we fell in a bundle of arms-n-legs and scattered towels onto the staircase that descended from our salon on the first floor. After a lot of grappling, tussling, pulling and scratching, she eventually managed to yank a gold signet ring from one of my fingers, and made off with it shouting, "If you want it back, you'll have to take me out!" Took her out, got it back, conclusion.

Nevertheless, a while before the advent of The Sandstorms, and prior to all the fun-n-frolics and promiscuous groupies, I had formed a small instrumental rock group at school. Unfortunately, we had no name, as far as I can't remember. Well, we probably did have a name, but it escapes me. Anyway, if it did have a name, it would probably have been Roger Ford and The Mustangs or something. I would have melted the Queen's crown down and sold the gold-n-jewels in order to own a Mustang Ford as mentioned in Chuck Berry songs. Lots of groups used the name of the singer, followed by the name of the backing band when choosing a name. Cliff Richard and The Shadows is an obvious one, and Johnny Kid and The Pirates is good, but some had a rather dubious linkage, for example, Johnny Jeep and the Four Wheel Drives. Then band names adopted two word titles like: The Beatles, The Hollies, The Who, The Bunch, The Searchers, The Bachelors, The Jerks, The Kinks, etc, and then progressed to single words like: Cream, Marmalade, Slade, Abba, Queen, etc.

I was a youngster, everybody was young (apart from old people), and like many of my enthusiastic, energised and creative generation, I had indulged in much guitar experimentation in the confines of the dining room at the back of my parents' bungalow. Guitar syndrome first manifested itself in the shape of a white acoustic, pick up clad/ hand-me-down guitar from my cousin Colin in Portsmouth. I really felt the bizz, couldn't play a sausage, and for a photo shoot with a Box Brownie camera in our drive, I donned a pair of smooth, darker than just dark glasses to complete the image. My next fatuous guitar

Homemade amp-n-speaker cabinets

romance was with a stunning, metallic greeny-blue Rosetti semi acoustic. Whilst travelling on the yellow number three bus through the village of Moordown, I'd spotted the object of my desire hanging amongst the grimy items in a second-hand shop. Squinting through the moist, teardrop pearly mist of condensation on the bus window, I would gaze down, longingly, frustrated to see the guitar languishing amongst so much discarded rubbish. I drooled at the thought of getting that beautifully contoured instrument into my grasp. In order to achieve ownership of such a, subjectively, desirable artefact, it would mean doing some serious persuasive work on my parents. A day or two on my best behaviour, sorted! I was in the car with my Mother and Father, and we were on our way to the second-hand emporium. Through youthful cunning and pathetic pleading, I had managed to convince them that it was the only thing I would ever ask for in my whole life, and I would never ask them for anything else, ever! Plus, I promised that I would help out at home in some way or other. Of course, that was a lie. The greeny-blue metallic Rosseti guitar sported a white plastic scratch board with two pickups and a couple of black control knobs. I studiously convinced my parents that the knobs were essential, but to be honest, at that stage I wasn't quite sure why.

All I needed was some kind of amplifier but I wasn't going to push my luck. Instead, I stripped down a disused Bakelite valve wireless, and using my undoubted electrical genius, managed to turn all its wiry circuitry innards into what passed for a guitar amplifier. That type of botching up method was nothing out of the ordinary for us youngsters in those days. We were always taking things apart and experimenting with potentially deadly substances and equipment that today would definitely attract a resounding 'no' from the faceless bureaucracy of Health and Safety. A typical example of our devil-may-care attitude would be November time when fireworks were readily available. Having done our stint of 'Penny for the Guy' outside the local newsagents (an old English tradition, now sadly ostracised to the annals of history), we would use the cash raised to buy fireworks, mainly penny bangers, and let me assure you that penny bangers were of some substance in those days. Utilising the masses of tools, work bench vice, furnace and anvil in my Father's workshop, my school friends and I, regaled in grey flannel shorts, with our white cotton shirtsleeves rolled up, would go to work like mad scientists. By emptying the gunpowder from bundles of penny bangers into a short piece of galvanised pipe, we could create one huge, mega banger of infinite proportions. A true Weapon of Mass Destruction. The excitement and anticipation of what destruction could be caused by such a thing was incredible, and we giggled-n-laughed as we conspiratorially poured the black gunpowder into the metal tube. Finally, by wedging the fuse in the end with a cork soaked in furniture glue, we were potential international terrorists. With great excitement, and more sniggering-n-spluttering caused by the thought of giving an old age pensioner a heart attack, off we would go to the test site ..... Cuckoo-Woods at the back of our house. From a relatively safe distance, under cover, so that we could still observe, we would lay, holding our breath, hearts thumping with anticipation, for the inevitable explosive outcome. The resulting eruption was never disappointing, and as far as I know, apart from minor injuries, dislodged school caps and dusty faces, none of us were ever killed. We also made dozens (a once perfectly adequate, but now discarded imperial measurement) of go-carts, but that's another story, mildly amusing, but nothing to do with rock groups. However, I sincerely believe that all the knee grazing boyish rough-n-tumble, in tandem with train sets and Meccano, all helped enormously to toughen us up and expand our practical abilities, character, and initiative – commodities imperative to rock stars.

Honeymoon over, and as a more diligent player, I progressed from the Rosetti guitar through a flurry of other solid electric, bizarrely shaped second-hand instruments that all ended up where they should have – firewood for old people in the winter. Eventually, I was playing something more honourable – a beautiful, brand new solid red VOX guitar from Germany. For amplification in those primeval days – and before my parents were totally convinced of my commitment to shell out for anything too expensive – the sound, or noises, went through an old cannibalised valve radio, and from there to separate speaker modules. Speaker modules? Ok, not quite that sophisticated. It was actually wired to two shoebox shaped cabinets containing two five inch round, plus one four inch, elliptical speakers. Entombed with my equipment in the back room at home, I sat hour after hour, day after night, guitar across lap, hunched over the gramophone, repeatedly replacing the needle (or stylus) with a crunch onto the 45rpm record. To achieve perfection, the correct chords and all the solo notes from the latest music, this was the laborious process that had to be endured before they could be played in the band. During our first gig – garbed in grey flannel shorts, white shirt and school tie – standing on the school hall stage (Wembley Stadium to us), I went completely Duane Eddy with the tremlo arm during 'Peter Gun', and tragedy struck. The spring system went twang and sent the whole caboodle collapsing in my hands. That traumatic incident led me – cradling the sad faulty product – back to the music shop with my Father (the one with the money and a score to settle for his son's début with the fine art of humiliation). Like many famous disasters, it morphed into a successful outcome. The owner of Minns Music shop (in an attempt to appease the situation, and my Father's wrath) pulled the slickest trick by producing an alternative instrument. It was an unforgettable, transforming moment when I found myself in the arms of a new, sleek, pinkie-red £150 Fender Stratocaster. It was stunning, and I was instantly bewitched by its subtle fingerboard action, luscious poppy red paint, and those beguiling, lustrous contours. Thus began a relationship, as aforementioned, which would last (even though I dallied with other beautiful models) throughout my life.

The Sandstorms' first booking

MY FRIEND DAVE and I were mad about the instrumental group The Ventures of America, The Spotnicks from Holland, and The Shadows, so the natural progression was that we decided to form our own instrumental group.

DAVE HITCHINGS was a childhood friend, and after the demise of The Sandstorms, we drifted apart for forty years, and then drifted back again. We were introduced to each other by our parents at the delicate age of twelve. Our first meeting followed the death of my best friend, Peter Watkins. Being an only son, I suppose it would be accurate to say that Peter had filled the role of surrogate brother. Peter and I were never apart, and therefore it was a great shock to lose him so young. Summer days were spent together rambling the safe countryside, making fires and secret camps in the woods and running over the heather-covered moorlands. Overnight, we camped out in our gardens in an Army surplus canvas ridge tent, and pushed each other around all over the village and beyond in homemade go-carts built with wooden orange boxes and old pram wheels. Having had the misfortune to watch him die slowly over a period of several months through which we exchanged hundreds of letters, all written in multicoloured pen, I came to the conclusion that he was a very brave and gallant person who I will always remember with great affection. The good die young because they are selected for a better place, whilst we have to stay and suffer what we deserve.

Dave was no taller than the shortest member of the group, and no shorter than the shortest. He was also no thinner than the thinnest and no thicker set than the thickest. He had the hairstyles of the time ..... DA, sideburns and quiff, later followed by mop top. (Isn't it sad; we took it for granted that we all had hair then and could bicker over one style or another, but now it's a novelty, or a wig.) Dave had a 'bird', as girlfriends were referred to then, and this situation filled me with a great deal of fascination, frustration and juvenile anxiety. Although I'd had a school boy crush on a girl named Lesley at Butlin's Holiday Camp in the seaside town of Clacton, and then came home and pined miserably for a fortnight, and previously developed an inept, childish flirtation with a fellow pupil called Lorna when I was in the infants school, I hadn't actually had a regular girlfriend. It was with the inquisitiveness of an awakening teenage boy that I pondered night-n-day over, "How come Dave had obtained a real live, 'Walkin Talking, Livin Doll' girlfriend, and one with all the grownup female lumps-n-bumps where they ought to be?" Most of all, the big question was, "How could I get one?"

My first instinct, and the simplest option to me, was to steal his. Instantly, I was aware that that plan was littered with the obvious, potentially tragic consequences. If caught perpetrating such a traitorous act, it could have caused a deal of male friction, not to mention the inevitable personal bone structural damage administered by Dave, and painful nose realignment, inflicted through such dastardly provocation. Overriding all was the destructive effect that such an action would have had on our budding rock group prospects, plus the absence of loyalty to a mate. Sometimes, the three of us, Dave, 'bird' and me, would sit in the back room of his parents' bungalow playing 'What'd I Say', a track on an LP by Ray Charles. Dave's girl and I would sit on the floor, alongside the twelve disc drop down stack Grundig record player, with me, the minstrel on acoustic guitar, being charming and discretely flirtatious, whilst accompanying Ray with that familiar piano intro. Whoever she was (it's been a long time) and I would sit there on the floor, singing along, "See the girl with the red dress on, well she can boogie-woogie all night long". Dave, however, the engineer, complacent that he had a girlfriend, sat up at his mother's wooden dining table, its oak surface scattered with millions of diminutive brass clock guts, like cogs, springs, and dead cuckoos, fiddling around with some intricate watch or time pacing mechanism. To aid his observation of this primitive, nanotechnology, Dave owned one of those jeweller's black plastic magnifying eye glasses, like a big thimble, that he managed, precariously, to grip in place over one of his eyes, in its socket. Observed with fascination by his bird and me, he achieved this miracle to hold it in place against the natural pull of gravity, by wrinkling up the skin around his eyelid to make folds, and scowling in a downward movement with his eyebrows. Very romantic! The bizarre process made him look like Ebenezer Scrooge pawing over his accounts, and was quite hideous and hilarious to me and his girl, and we just fell about, convulsed with laughter, like we were being tickled, holding our stomachs, unable to speak. "What are you two laughing at?" Dave would respond, irritably. "It was just some words in the song, Dave." Of course, we played other tracks, but that's the one I remember and still play.

Some Friday or Saturday nights, the three of us would jump on-n-off various numbered buses en route to local band venues. There we made notes as to what the different bands were playing, and obviously enjoyed the ambience of the evening and dancing together. Some of the tunes that I remember bands playing were 'Return To Sender' by Elvis and ironically, 'The Girl Of My Best Friend'! On the way home, we might stop at the Milk Bar in Post Office Road for a Knickerbocker Glory. This delicacy was served in a very tall, cone shaped, vase like glass, and contained a mouth-watering layered plethora of syrup, pink-n-white ice cream, and tinned fruit, all topped off with squirts of synthetic cream, brown chocolate dye, a red glace cherry, and fan shaped crispy wafer. (Another symbol of the age.) A very long spoon was required to attack such a thing. Alternatively if we were returning from say, The Burlington in Boscombe, it would be the Wimpy Bar for a 'Bender' (a dissected sausage). I wonder what happened to the bird? I wonder what happened to the Knickerbocker Glory?

FROM CONCEPTION, Dave and I never harboured any doubt or question as to whether or not either of us could actually play a guitar. We just decided we were now a group, with the naive innocence that the rest would just fall into place. I elected myself as lead guitar, so Dave bought a guitar to compliment me as rhythm, but after a while found that he couldn't play it. We were obviously going nowhere with that set up, so we decided that he would try drums. Together, we devised a rather devilish but brilliantly elementary strategy designed to save us from another waste of money. Both of us, being of such a delicate early teen-age (thirteen), we only had our meagre pocket money, plus my supplement of ten shillings a week from a Saturday job as an employee in my uncle's ironmongers. Even so, and even all together, we had nowhere near enough dosh to purchase a full drum set. That being the case, we decided to mobilize our devious plot. Furtively, like two secret agents on a special mission, Dave and I travelled to Winton on the number three yellow bus. Alighting from the bus at the Winton Banks stop, we entered the consecrated portal and hall of the nearby Church Youth Club. For the first twenty minutes or so, we played billiards with an old chap who went by the nickname of Sunshine. Sunshine was an unkempt old bloke and a bit of a local character, the butt of kids' and grownups' jokes. He suffered with a walking impediment and would often be seen shuffling around Winton clutching a shabby old shopping bag. On youth club nights, Sunshine would always be in attendance, up on the stage teaching kids how to play billiards. As youngsters do, we smirked at his overgrown nasal and ear hairs, and the tufts of grey bristle that he'd missed out shaving, going up-n-down on his protruding Adam's apple. Our parents warned us that he was a bit odd, and if he tried anything, we should apply a quick knee to the groin. I don't ever remember him being anything but a decent, courteous old bloke, helpful and always with a good word.

Once we felt sure that we had blended in, and that everyone else was occupied with ping pong, darts or sorting old shoes and jumpers into bags for Ethiopia, we casually replaced our billiard cues in their respective racks. Surreptitiously, Dave and I entered the musty smelling vestry, closed the door behind us, and quickly got to work. I removed a three foot square ply board panel to reveal the entrance leading to the space below the wooden stage. Together, we slithered into the fusty, dark storage space. Crawling-n-scratching around in the dank, dusty cobwebbed gloom, we fumbled around in the filth until we came across a large bass drum belonging to the Boys Brigade Marching Band. Having dragged the monstrous thing outside into the dark alleyway, conspiratorially – whilst trying unsuccessfully to stifle our spluttering youthful gaffors – we scurried, like sewer rats, along the side of the church building, bass drum clutched between us, out into the high street, along the pavement and straight onto a yellow double-decker bus that just happened to be at the bus stop at the right time. The drum was emblazoned with the Boys Brigade insignia in gold, white and blue paint. Camouflage was necessary, so it was treated by Dave and me to a very hasty and inexpert paint job; nobody would ever have recognised it again. Dave bought a selection of drum sticks (snare, timpani, brushes) even 'though we had no idea what we needed, and started banging on it. To our disillusion, it just went boom, boom, boom, boom, boom...boom. Without the accompaniment of bugles, a crashing cymbal and a platoon of soldiers' boots crunching along behind him, it just wasn't rock-n-roll. Even so, it had the desired effect, and it wasn't long before his parents (and some disgruntled neighbours) couldn't stand the constant booming any longer. The bass drum was cleaned, stealthily returned to the church (presumably no-one had noticed its absence, and it would be there ready for the next church parade), and Dave's parents bought him a brand new 'Premier' drum kit. Dave's drums also came from Minns Music in Gervis Place, Bournemouth. Like all the other young musicians, we would frequent all the local music shops every Saturday to hang around discussing all the latest chart music and gigs with the other musicians. If a guitarist had learnt some new techniques, they would show it off, and inevitably, everyone else would copy it. Our main objective was to scrutinise and try out all the latest instruments, amps and drum kits. A music shop, full of instruments, guitars and such hanging around the walls, and all those flashy cubes of powerful sound equipment was, and still is, intoxicating to an addict, like an Aladdin's Cave. It's almost a place of worship, and in some cases, a place of craftsmanship. There was also Eddie Moors music shop in Boscombe, Don Strikes in Westbourne, and Achille Roma in Parkstone. If we took a fancy to, say, the latest VOX amplifier, Eddie would say, "Take it and try it on a gig." Obviously, that was too much to refuse, so we took him up on it, and more often than not, it would result in a sale because we couldn't bear to hand the kit back. Eddie Moors, Minns Music, Don Strikes and Achille Roma went on to be major musical instrument suppliers in the area for many years.

TO COMPLETE THE GROUP, we needed more members, so a mate – and Shadow fanatic – Mike Brown, didn't need too much encouragement to become our bass player. Mike was tall with a physique like a rasher of bacon, and blessed with a shock of spiky blonde locks. Hailing from Parley Cross, near Ferndown, he lived with his family. They were all regular church attendees, as were most of us then, including practically all of the rest of the population. Did it make us better people? Who knows, but I'm sure there was definitely a certain innocence and self-discipline ingrained. Mike was a keen train spotter, and an ardent photographer. In fact, most kids were interested in trains then, most probably because there were still many of those thrilling, puffing, chuffing, coal burning, steaming, riveted beasts rattling along the steel rails. A little train spotting book could purchased from the newsagent in which to record the names, serial numbers and types of trains spotted. There would always be a group of youngsters, mainly boys in school uniform and mackintoshes, gathered on the end of the station platform, ogling over these clanking iron monsters. Herein lays a tenuous link with rock-n-roll and trains. Some of those driving chunky rhythms-n-blues of rock were very close to the sound of a moving train. Indeed, Muddy Waters' early compositions sprung from the strains of the wailing trains. The Six Five Special fifties pop show on TV that had all our eyeballs glued to the tiny cathode ray tube screen for the duration, opened spectacularly with a rip-roaring, driving, thrusting song, and a stunning black-n-white film, from the driver on the footplates point of view, of a steam train rushing over the points, hurtling through pitch black tunnels, swishing past blurred signal boxes ..... wow! Brilliant.

Mike was a connoisseur, and studied The Shadows closely and possessed all the records they ever made. He scrutinised every note and was terribly precious about accuracy. If I dared so much as play a single bum note in any Shadows' composition, he would ridicule me with some sardonic, stinging comment like, "Sorry Rog, but that's the worst version of 'Apache' I've ever heard in my life, and if you think I'm going to stand on a stage with you playing like that, you've seriously got me wrong." None of us would ever argue with that point of view because, like him, we were all sticklers for accuracy and a slick, professional presentation.

Fortunately for us, **TONY HABERFIELD** replied to an advert that we had placed in the Bournemouth Echo for a rhythm guitarist. Tony was polite, reliable, courteous, and shorter-n-stockier in stature than long lean Mike, but made up for it with his effervescent personality. He was always, apart from when he wasn't, laughing at something in a pressure cooker way. It started with him panting-n-hissing through his teeth like the sound of a bicycle pump, going red in the face, and finally exploding with a mighty roar. Thinking back, we all seemed to be laughing at anything and nothing most of the time. He auditioned for Dave and me in the front room of his home in Tuckton, near Christchurch. We were both suitably amazed by his slick, smooth guitar technique, and to prove his commitment to music, he had actually manufactured his own guitar out of scrap wood. Later, he purchased a fine red Fender-like guitar and Vox thirty watt amp, and that completed our Fender Vox line up. Tony was very familiar with all the Buddy Holly numbers which he could sing brilliantly. He had a good bluesy-n-rock voice for Chuck Berry and Little Richard stuff, but could also slip comfortably into more melodic, ballad type numbers. His guitar playing was inspirational and heavily influenced by the likes of Big Bill Broonzy, Leadbelly, Muddy Waters and Bob Dylan. Tony was definitely in The Sandstorms. Sadly, some thirty years later, I heard that Tony had died, not long after his sister was killed in the London, Clapham train disaster. I believe they were very close and it had a dramatic effect on him.

Finally, **JOSS** (don't know where he came from?) was on vocals. Joss was a waiter in the Pullman restaurant car on the 'Bournemouth Belle' steam train that travelled from Bournemouth to London. With Joss on board, resplendent in his livery uniform, pandering to his silver service passengers' every culinary need, the train chuff-chuffed, billowing its comforting, curling smoke, there-n-back twice every day. That being the case, on our way to gigs, we had to stop and pick up Joss (following his last shift) from the Bournemouth Central Railway Station. Joss had a good voice, stage presence and he looked real good. Unfortunately, Joss was of a delicate nature, and sadly, after the Moose Hall gig in Christchurch, he decided to leave.

THE MOOSE HALL GIG was one of those notorious occasions that was destined to go down in the chronicles of Sandstorms' history. Fundamentally, without beating about the bush, for the first three quarters of the evening,

The Sandstorms with Joss

everything was going fine. Our small but reliable bunch of fans were present and contentedly dancing to 'The Twamp' and generally enjoying our renditions of all the latest hits. Now I must create the historic image of the dancers. For a start, everyone hung around against the two side walls – blokes on one side, and the girls on the other. A lot of snorting and giggling and eyeing-up took place from a safe distance. Boys would usually join forces with a mate for support, and pick out two girls with the prospect of approaching them together. That kind of tactic felt safer, and any sneering female rejection could be laughed off together, perhaps with asides of, "I didn't like mine anyway," backed up with, "No, I didn't like yours either." Once the rock group began to play, all the girls would drift onto the floor and begin to dance (adopting that old classic pose and much clichéd ritual) around their handbags. The fashion image was late fifties/ early sixties. Girls generally favoured those enormous bouffant hair styles. Many of these 'bouffants' incorporated expertly coiffured French pleats. These were created by rolling the hair from the nape of the neck to the crown of the head, and then holding it all in place with a thousand Kirby grips and pins. The top was then furiously back-combed as high as a skyscraper, and finally all glued in place with copious amounts of stiff lacquer. Girls' dresses were shift-type jobs, or pencil line tight skirts with knees stuck together. Later, they were to move skyward to become, the Mini skirt. Smashing! Stiletto heels were still quite common, but obviously not always popular with dance floor owners. In fact, in some venues with expensive wooden floors, stilettos were banned, so girls often danced barefoot, and even if they weren't banned, they still danced barefoot, presumably because their shoes were so uncomfortable. Within the animal species, as is often the case, it's the male who appears as the strutting peacock with all the colourful attractive features for flashing at a potential mate. However, the human species is generally quite the opposite. It's the female who wears the refinements of colour and war paint to attract. So what we saw at the Moose Hall and other venues of that era was no different. Female eyes, resplendent with long fluttering false eyelashes, were carefully outlined with thick, black kohl pencil eyeliner. The rest of the face was heavily encrusted with thick greasy layers of pan-stick (unfriendly to men's shirt collars), all held in place with plentiful amounts of sneeze-inducing neutral powder. The finishing piece de resistance was the prolific application of pale, pinkie-white lipstick. Judgement of the males attributes were delicately summed up in depth by the girls with, "D'ya fancy 'im?"

Suddenly, and seemingly without warning, the civility of the Moose Hall evening was totally dashed. The friendly ambience changed from calm, to pure, unadulterated naked aggression. From our elevated vantage point, performing on the stage, we could see straight over the heads of the dancers, and right to the back of the hall, where, in the confines of the narrow entrance, cloakroom area and toilets, an almighty punch-up was erupting. At the root of the problem was a bunch of gate-crashing greasers. (I think they had decided not to pay the entry fee of three shillings and sixpence.) A small green baized card table, positioned next to the entrance with the money and tickets on, was their first target. It was violently flipped up and sent flying, cash, ticket stubs-n-all into the air. Trying to be as oblivious and nonchalant as possible, we played on whilst my Father (our manager) and Dave's Mother (a fearsome, five foot nothing Scott with the snarling, aggressive temperament of a Jack Russell) fought a fist-n-chair fight with the greasers. One of the leather clad rockers managed to break through the flailing, punching, screaming parent barricade, roughly elbowed his way through the dancers, ultimately clambering up, via a chair, onto the stage, brandishing an empty beer bottle. The grimacing vandal then proceeded to smash the bottle on the metal rim of Dave's tom-tom drum. The band was under no illusions that he was obviously intent on doing us some serious bodily harm. Rather like the band on The Titanic, we were still playing, and to the sound of crunching broken slivers of glass under our chukka boots, were even prancing out The Shadows' Walk. I suppose, subconsciously, I was under the erroneous impression that the thug would perhaps spot the dancers, feel vulnerable, realise the futility of his mission, put the jagged, broken bottle down and join in.

Realistically, and having noticed the villain's sunken, dead piercing eyes and snarling top lip, I knew that wishful scenario was definitely not going to happen. However, as luck would have it, and we had it, and before Goliath could hack Dave's throat-n-face out with his ghastly, savage looking weapon, he was repelled by Dave who took a couple of beats out of 'Walk Don't Run' and stabbed the lunging menace in the eye with his drum stick. Just to make sure, and strictly in time with the music, Dave cracked him over the head with a single maraca .... "Cha, cha, cha!" shouted Dave. This action appeared to give the audience the go-ahead to retaliate, and after a few minutes of flying fists and chairs, saw the thugs, to the last man, gone. Somebody suggested that the wounded chap, now sporting only one eye, went on to become Johnny Kidd, lead singer with the Pirates. For anyone who doesn't know, whilst performing with The Pirates, Johnny wore a black patch over one eye. Apparently, or so folklore would have it, Johnny was tuning his guitar one day when a string broke and it whipped back into his eye. Whilst the eye was healing, he wore a black eye patch. It seemed to be a good image idea, so he continued to wear the patch and thus they became Johnny Kid and The Pirates. Well why not? The truth is so boring. Although gallantly, we (Dave, Mike and I) had all stood our ground and remained defiantly on stage, Joss, still singing brilliantly, but understandably reluctant to draw himself to the attention of the thug, had moved delicately into the wings where he discreetly vanished behind the moth-eaten curtain. He was never seen again.

SPACE TRAVEL and satellites orbiting the globe, although a possibility, had not yet been achieved during our pre-pubescence, and therefore were merely dreams confined to our childish cerebral matter. Before the advent of TV and electronic home entertainment, children attended Saturday morning pictures. For me, it was at The Modern cinema in Winton (later to become the proverbial, Bingo Hall). The majority of films were 'Cowboys and Indians', projected in black-n-white, and possessed the hypnotic power to transport us wide-eyed school kids into a fantastic world of make-believe. Enthralling characters such as, The Lone Ranger and Tonto, Robin Hood and his Merry Band of Men, and Roy Rogers and his trusty horse Trigger were just a few that got our legs, still too short to touch the floor, swinging-n-kicking the seat in front with anticipation. Films were serialised, and so we had to wait, frustrated, until the following Saturday morning, in order to discover whether or not the goody or the bady who was left, desperately clinging by his fingernails, would eventually fall into the precipice, or slide screaming, with the whole cinema cheering to see him getting his just deserts, into a hungry grinding mincer. The other film category that we found most fascinating and invigorating was space travel. Of course, the spacemen, who shuffled stiltedly and robotically from behind huge boulders in dusty disused quarries, lacked the sophisticated special effects and computer graphics that we have all now become used to, and come to expect. In retrospect, they were obviously wearing vacuum cleaner parts, including the cardboard box they came in. But to me, they were real aliens. I mention all this twaddle for a pertinent reason. One evening, an instrumental group called The Spotnicks emerged from Holland and appeared on Top Of The Pops. Eye-bogglingly, they were all attired in realistic looking 'Michelin Man' spacesuits, big globular upside-down goldfish bowls on their heads, and playing Fender guitars with their inimitable flurry of orbital electronic effects. I was completely smitten. Hence, within days, or more probably hours, The Sandstorms rock group were playing items such as 'Happy Hendriks Polka', 'Orange Blossom Special', 'Moonshot', 'Amapola', etc., from the LP 'Out-a Space The Spotniks in London'.

The Sandstorms fact: our first booking was a Dr Barnardo's dance, and the second was a staff function at The South Western Hotel, now non-existent, opposite Bournemouth Central Railway Station.

Due to Joss's untimely and rather sad departure, Dean Fane (a devout Cliff Richard disciple) joined the band. He looked good – tall, lean, brushed back dark hair

The Sandstorms with Dean Fane

and wore some slick, white mohair suits. Dean was Cliff, and always has been. He could sing (important for a vocalist) but most of all, and to prove that he was serious, he owned a real good PA system. It had two attractive grey, stereo column speakers and a nice compact sound-desk on wire legs. Dean was dedicated to his singing, knew every Cliff song, looked and moved like him and obviously belonged to the Cliff Richard Fan Club. He ate-n-drank the same, and sung 'Move it' like the master. During his time with The Sandstorms, he couldn't find a day job that suited him. His predicament caused us a lot of amusement. He seemed to have a string of driving jobs for firms such as Wall's Ice Cream, and Miller's Pies. Talking of pies, Dean once had a job at The Triangle, Bournemouth, serving customers in a haberdashery shop. During his first lunch hour, the boss, a devout orthodox Jew, wandered into the staff room for a chat. After a few minutes, he asked Dean what he was munching on. "A pork pie," declared Dean, unaware of the gaff. "Mmm, very nice!" The boss's face turned puce, and with his mouth foaming like a mating camel, he fired poor old Dean (spluttering his pie) on the spot, and warned him not to darken his haberdashery doorstep again.

There was a fair amount of friction at gigs in those days – remember the Mods and Rockers? There was also a certain amount of latent, not so friendly rivalry between the local groups. We had a couple of gigs disrupted by the rougher elements of a rival band and their fans or thug base. A typical incident was whilst performing on stage at the Corn Exchange, Blandford, and enjoying the pleasant ambiance and sight of the dancers doing 'The Mashed Potato' to our music, when a load of yobs (headed by the lead guitarist of another band) barged in. They were well tanked up, jeering and throwing insults at us from the back of the hall. Stoically, we played on, trying to ignore their territorial malevolence, and encouraged by our devoted public and bunch of fans who were putting up a good reverse verbal slanging match in our defence. Inevitably that only served to fan the flames and provoke the flight of missiles (bottles-n-glasses) overhead and onto the stage, and ultimately, onto us. Fortunately, it soon seemed to fizzle out, leaving a few black eyes, smashed chairs, torn clothes and broken teeth. These incidents were fortunately few, and never a big problem.

The Sandstorms, Pavilion

VENUES AND BOOKINGS WERE WHERE WE NEEDED TO BE,

and ultimately, The Sandstorms had a residency at the Pavilion Ballrooms in Bournemouth. It was a lovely, sophisticated, well decorated and comfortable venue to play. Re-opened in 1934 after major refurbishment and additional buildings, it was beautifully designed and ornately adorned with gold leaf filigree on the coving, ceiling roses and art deco/Roman-style columns. For The Sandstorms, it was always full to the gunwales with young revellers, all energised and anxious to get some serious dancing-n-dating in. It had a brilliant sprung wooden dance floor and boasted a very well stocked, pleasant, long, curvaceous bar, situated directly behind the whole length of the wide stage. In the adjoining Pavilion Theatre, artists such as Kenneth Williams (appearing in Loot by Joe Orton), Dick Emery, Tony Hancock and Arthur Haynes were appearing in stage productions. The Sandstorms performed there every Tuesday on Beat Nights and again on Saturday evenings. This meant that we were fortunate enough to work alongside many local, semi and famous bands of the era, i.e. The Moody Blues, The Bachelors, Manfred Man, The Who, etc. The Pavilion was one of our better paid jobs at thirty quid. However, we were presented with a challenge. Long corridors ran down both sides of The Pavilion, from the front entrance and foyer, all the way to the ballroom at the back. Dragging all our amps-n-kit down these long passageways on a regular basis proved to be a bit of a slog. To overcome this problem, and utilising the skills we gained designing go-carts, we cut some ply board rectangles, about three by two, screwed casters on each of the four corners, stood the amps on them, and literally wheeled all the kit to the stage. Simple.

Charlie, Sandstorms' Manager

We also played the 45 Club situated at the Triangle Bournemouth, twenty quid. Our manager, Charlie Downton, opened the 45 Club with a business partner, and with the help of members of The Sandstorms, we turned a scruffy old upstairs, dilapidated storeroom, into a slightly less scruffy and dog-eared club. Charlie was a bit of a character, middle-aged, medium height, slicked back slightly thinning dark hair, who always had a big cigar, in his chops, or rolling between his fingers. Bit of a snazzy dresser was Charlie, and like his personality, wore some pretty flamboyant outfits. Typical garb would consist of chukka boots of various colours. He once gave a pair to The Bachelors after some fans sneaked into the dressing room and nicked theirs. I surmise that he must have driven home in his socks? He sported several silver-n-gold silk suits with tapered trousers, jacket and waistcoat, complimented with a puffy, silver fleck car coat, and fake black Astrakhan collar. He was fit, tough, gregarious, with a quick wit and sharp intellect, and was extremely altruistic ….. when Mike the bass joined, he didn't have the correct, matching amplifier, so Charlie went out and bought him a brand new Vox. (Though he had to give it back when he left.) Charlie was also our manager, and made sure that we were performing regularly and getting into the venues that needed to be got into. The Sandstorms was his prize band, and he constantly carried our portfolio around in his light brown leather brief case, ready to whip out, like a cowboy's six-gun, and thrust under the nose of any potential dude booker.

The Sandstorms

I suggested to Charlie that it would be a good idea to fill the 45 Club with sofas and comfortable armchairs, rather than the usual nothing, or hard splinter ridden wooden furniture found in some of the other venues. He agreed that it was a good idea and so all The Sandstorms drove around town, chatting to girls, picking up old armchairs and flea-infested sofas in Charlie's trailer, dragged them up the two flights of stairs, and scattered them all around the club. My suggestion wasn't purely for comfort. There was an ulterior motive. In the darkness of the club, armchairs and sofas were a much better vehicle to get in some serious snogging. After a period of time, of which I'm not too sure, one year, two years? the other bloke, whoever he was? bought Charlie out. Eventually, it became Bumbles Club, where some thirty years later I performed as a visiting, 'Fabulous London Cabaret Act', as described in the newspaper. Vic Allen, local agent to The Sandstorms in the sixties, had booked my London based speciality act, completely unaware of the serendipitous connection. It was an enlightening indication of just how fickle agents, newspapers and jolly old Joe Public can be. Because I had moved to London (the entertainment capital), and the venue in Bournemouth didn't realize that originally I was an indigenous local, the London connection gave me extra kudos and a fancy billing in my own town. Pathetic.

Charlie's overriding motive for being happily bought out of the 45 Club was because he had opened another music venue, The Savoy Rooms, in Midsummer Norton, Somerset. It was a good old traditional ballroom with a big proscenium arch stage and grand spacious sprung dance floor. It proved a most lucrative move for Charlie, in fact he was held up one night whilst driving back to Bournemouth with all the night's takings bagged up in his car. On a windy, deserted, pitch-black stretch of country road, a mysterious car pulled out, blocking the narrow carriageway. It was instantly obvious that whoever they were, they knew that Charlie took the same route every night with the cash. Not one to suffer fools and highwaymen gladly, he managed, miraculously, to turn his car around one hundred and eighty degrees. It was then facing the robber's car boot-n-rear bumper end first. Naturally, as Charlie leaned out of the side window and looked back, he saw the bandits standing by their car. They appeared to be bemused as to what was going on. Before they had time to organise a brain cell between them, Charlie slammed his toe on the accelerator, and with the acrid burning tyre rubber permeating his nostrils, he reversed backwards at high speed. The villains scattered as he clipped the rear lightest end of their vehicle, slewing it off the road. Affecting a few vital frantic twists of the steering wheel, Charlie, together with his bags of cash, managed to make good an escape, triumphantly disappearing, enveloped into the dark night. We played Midsummer Norton many times to a good, happy and responsive audience, and enjoyed many shattered late night post gig drives home. We were never held up.

Eddie, Tony, and Roger

There was also The Downstairs Club at the Lansdowne. It was below the shops, hence the name, and owned in the sixties by Jerry Stooks, a gregarious man of much vigour and eccentricity. He went on to start one of the first Kissagram agencies in the area, in healthy competition with another Kissagram agency run by his contemporary, Dave Woodbury Entertainments. Jerry could often be seen clucking, hen-like (hence Hen Nights?) around the town in a yellowy-reddish chicken costume ...... yeah, well!! Then it became The New Lansdowne Jazz Club (Jerry had his own jazz band), and (perhaps he bought a disco kit?) then Le Disque a Go! Go! We played there often. It really had a rock-n-roll, sleazy, rustic club atmosphere. A good description would be to compare it with the famous Cavern Club in Liverpool. The walls and the low claustrophobic red brick ceiling were built in a series of ancient, crumbling arches. In fact, it resembled a small section from a Victorian sewer, without the excrement. Whenever the place was packed, hip-to-shoulder with rocking punters dancing to loud throbbing groups, it became hot, damp-n-steamy like a rain forest. Electrifying! The entrance to The Downstairs Club was upstairs, squeezed in a narrow gap between two shops. One entered the scruffy looking establishment (oozing character to us) straight from the pavement. Whilst standing, fidgeting in the queue to pay, the stimulating dull thudding sound of the band below would reverberate up the dingy, ragged wooden staircase and cause everyone to move-n-sway gently to the rhythm. Eventually, our impatience would be rewarded when the usher opened the door. Eager, and bursting with youthful pent up anticipation, the teenage scrum would surge forward with the terrifying velocity of an ancient battering ram. By then an unstoppable force, we would all descend on the narrow, gloomy staircase that had been built into a gangway that resembled a mine shaft. Whooping-n-squealing, our bundle of vibrant youthful humanity clattered on down the dozen or so creaky steps until we reached the first landing. The whole sensation was like being in the Haunted House at the fun-fair. After negotiating a very squashy sharp left and tramping down a few more groaning steps with the decaying white distemper from the damp walls soiling our arms, we made the final descent, eventually arriving in the throbbing, vibrant den of iniquity. Still on the move (but now composed with a slower, smooth, sauntering girl-pulling gait), and in order to afford ourselves a little more comfort in that airless calaboose, we would slip off our jackets and casually (Jack-the-Ladish) toss them onto the huge mound of discarded coats, shoes and bags that lay under the stairs which passed as the cloakroom. Dave, Mike, Tony and I grabbed drinks from the rough wooden structure, professing to be a bar, and together, clutching the unique, knobbly, hip-shaped glass Coca-Cola bottles with their dark fizzy liquid content, in our sweaty fists, we shoved our way through the throng, arrogantly enough to impress, but not enough to start a fight, till we arrived at the edge of the low stage, close up to the band.

All evening, I would be mesmerised, with my eyes glued to the guitarist's nimble fingers. Amongst others, The Thunderbirds were a favourite group; in particular, I was smitten with their version of 'Stormy Monday', not that I'm all that much into Blues itself. I enjoy some of it, and have seen Gary Moore and played his 'Still Got The Blues' which has to be up there, wherever that is, as one of the most inspired guitar solos ever devised. However, I find the Blues in general can get a bit pretentious, and some musicians like to disclaim their real roots i.e. Chuck Berry, Duane Eddy, The Shadows, purely out of snobbery, to be associated with the Blues, disclaiming themselves from a lot of culturally important, mainstream material. Once I had memorised some new chords, or a sharp sounding solo riff, I would be out of there, up the stairs and home on the next available bus. Before bed, I would incarcerate myself in the back room with my guitar, volume low so as not to wake the neighbours, and before there was any chance of me forgetting everything I had seen, I would put all that newly discovered information into practice.

AND THE BURE CLUB where we were on the bill with Cilla Black of 'Anyone Who Had a Heart' and 'You're My World' fame, and of course many more

memorable hits that I can't call to mind just now. Cilla wore that sixties wedge-shaped hairstyle, tapered sharply into the neck, the uneven sides, one short and one long, sweeping forwards over the ears, ending tight alongside the cheeks. Oh yeah, and the teeth. The Bure Club was an old converted stable block with the horse stalls and smatterings of straw retained inside. Its crude state wasn't for trendy effect, just lack of cash, or more probably just couldn't be bothered. Whatever, it didn't matter, they were used as intimate (good for snogging) cubicle-type seating areas. That night, we aired 'The Hall Of The Mountain King', Decca label (what a wealth of information) by Nero and The Gladiators instrumental group. It received a ripple of applause from a teenage audience, so I suppose we done good, and it was worth the hours of practice, worn down plectrums and blistered fingers. Any road up, it worked, so it stayed in. The place was a bit grubby, but then most of the venues were grubby. Anywhere upstairs, or in a cellar, and with not too many neighbours, was game for a club. Rough-n-ready to rock was the only criteria. Seedy-n-squalid would be an accurate way to describe the state of many clubs, and yet, for some inconceivable reason, we hark back to their smoky, slimy griminess with fondness and melancholy ..... well, that was the novelty of it. Some management's idea was to get as many heaving sweaty bodies in their club as was physically possible. There was often no thought of comfort or personal safety by the administrators, and because lots of us took advantage by going in on one ticket, and then opening the fire escape door for all our mates to flood in, the fire escape door would be nailed up. What Health and Safety?

THERE WERE MANY STRANGE VENUES, including The Star Inn, Ringwood. We were often booked there, performing in what at first sight would seem to be a long narrow potting shed with cold grey flagstone floor. This strange building was separated from the pub by a small, *not* very attractive, stinking dustbin littered backyard. The roof of this potting shed structure was like an old neglected greenhouse with its paint peeling wooden rafters. At the far end, there was a small platform/stage for the band with a door at the other end where people would wander in from the pub. It was always cold to start with, and playing an instrument with cold fingers is never conducive to a good, enjoyable performance. However, after an hour or so – like with most pub gigs – the punters got well-oiled. Nearby, there was a new Ringwood by-pass under construction. Gangs of jolly navies from the road workings would be in abundance during The Star Inn gigs, sporting waistcoats, brass buckled belts, cloth caps, rolled up shirtsleeves, and grey flannel trousers; the term 'ragged rascals' would be a good description. One of them even came with bare feet! After a few pints, invariably a squabble would break out between two, three, four or more, and the inevitable punch-up would ensue. It was always sparked off by some trivial matter, like a spilt drink, or an indiscreet glance at another man's girl. Grinning with amusement, we always managed to play on untouched, and pleased that we weren't the subject of their pent-up aggression. By last orders (as it was in those prehistoric times) they wanted more-n-more music to accompany their alcoholically induced, wobbly legged gesticulating frenzy of frenetic dancing and blood curdling whoops-n-screams. Our reply was to give them our sweaty twenty minute version of 'Twist and Shout', and the thirty minute marathon, 'Johnny B Goode'. When the landlord finally appeared to flick on the strip-lights, and pay us our ten pound fee, it killed the atmosphere stone dead, bringing the smoky, rocking potting shed gig to a horrible, stark, sobering finish. As we packed up, a drunken middle-aged American man with a face full of whiskey would regularly stagger over and tell us, through slurred drink fumed breath, "Hey you guys, the electronics are good." We never knew exactly what he meant, but we took it as a compliment, and used the expression for anything that was good to us young men, even referring to girls.

ALSO, THERE WAS THE WINTER GARDENS, with its outstanding

acoustics, an ideal venue for The Bournemouth Symphony Orchestra. A brave-n-gallant battle was fought by a local action group to retain it for the orchestra, but inevitably it succumbed to cash driven development and council bureaucracy, and was thus sadly demolished. Another strong case to keep it was that as a schoolboy, I sang there in the choir with the Bournemouth Symphony Orchestra, conducted by the renowned and most prestigious, Sir Charles Groves. No? Just thought I'd throw it in. Appearing on the Winter Gardens stage as The Sandstorms was fun and made one feel very important, grandiose, and for those few precious, rewarding and unrepeatable moments of our lives, made us the main focus of interest. The Winter Gardens stage was splendid for a performer, wide, open and deep, with high tiered seating in an oval, rising up behind the stage, amphitheatre-like for big do's, rather like the Albert Hall. After a loudmouthed, enthusiastically flattering big build-up introduction from our gushing, over-the-top compere, we strutted majestically from the wings, confidently swaggering across the stage towards our amps-n-drums, bathing indulgently in the tumultuous applause, guitars slung nonchalantly over our shoulders, imitating the rock stars we were striving to be. It gave one an elevated feel, and just a smidgen of power. We rocked hard on that stage that night, and with the audience-n-fans well and truly behind us, we eventually made our exit into the wings, leaving the stage splattered with our sweat. Even later at the Chinese restaurant, still on a high, chewing on our 'coming down after a good gig meal' and Champagne (Pomeroy) guzzling, plus the proverbial debrief (who did good and who should have done better stuff), we still had the sound of the audience's appreciative, resounding applause ringing in our young ears.

The Winter Gardens

AND The Wheel House (big church hall type place, high stage and a room downstairs from what I remember), The Ritz, The Exeter Hotel, The Y.M.C.A. Cavern Club, The Cat and Canary, Kinson Community Centre, Starlight, The Burlington, The Woodman, Club Rio, The Half Way (full of rockers), The Woodlands, The Blue Boar, Rockley Sands, The Park Ballroom Above Bar Southampton, The Mowlem Theatre Swanage, The Pavilion Weymouth, and everywhere else, pubs-n-hotels that used live bands at the time we were playing. I have a newspaper cutting from The Bournemouth Times, written by Ken Bailey, that announces, 'The Sandstorms celebrate their four hundredth gig tonight at The Royal Ballrooms, Boscombe'. Avenue Artists' agency Southampton gave us the gigs at the Ballrooms, where we were intriguingly billed, 'Teenbeat Rock-n-Twist to The Sandstorms'. It had a serious 'Come Dancing' ballroom downstairs, with the resident Bill Collins big band for serious ballroom dancers, and upstairs there was a rock room, with a high stage in the centre of one side of the room for pop bands like us. It felt important and special to play there. Groups important to us performed in the rock room of The Royal Ballrooms, so that when we were on that stage, treading the boards of our rock heroes, it made us feel very special, and more than a little bit puffed up with ourselves. They paid fifteen pounds. The Royal Ballrooms previous life was as The Hippodrome and featured hundreds of the speciality acts, dancers, magicians and comedians of the era. Stars, such as The Cheeky Chappie, Max Miller, would appear there on a regular basis, to the delight of local patrons, including my parents and me.

Mike the bass left the band after one of our Ballrooms' gigs to join the Navy, so it was all very touching. We said our fond fare thee wells, shook hands, and as a token of our affection, we all chipped in and bought him a half glass of shandy. Charlie paid him, minus the shandy. Mike left the Ballrooms a lonely solitary figure carrying his dark guitar case. The double barred fire exit doors slammed closed behind him, and for forty odd years, we never saw him again. We also worked the Ballrooms' gig with one of our hero groups, my cousin's band, Mike Devon and The Diplomats from Portsmouth.

HAIR STYLES WERE IMPORTANT

HAIR STYLES WERE IMPORTANT and classified everyone as a particular type, or group. Predominantly, it matched a taste in clothes, music, culture, food, drink and art. Hair design and cut defined you as a Mod, Rocker, Hippy, Beatnik or tramp. The fifties and sixties saw a revolution in hair fashion. Ladies hair stylists such as Raymond's (Mr Teasy-Weasy), Fidel Sassoon and French of London introduced amazing new lines for women, and somehow, men's hair fashion followed, but mainly due to the influence of rock-n-pop artists. For men, there was the DA (ducks arse), Tony Curtis and Elvis quiff. It replaced the traditional war time 'short-back-and-sides' and 'a bit off the top', usually topped with lashings of Brillcream. The Beatles went from mop tops to long haired bearded jobs. Being precocious, I would frequent my own personal choice of barber by the name of Roberto. He was a short, dark, hairy armed, woman appreciating Italian, and with much fake servile posturing, diligence and care, created the hip of styles.

Dean, Dave and Bachelor

The Sandstorms with The Bachelors

TO SOME OF OUR ELDERS (who had fought and nearly died in the War) The Rolling Stones (formed in nineteen sixty two) were just long haired yobs. "Put em in the Army", they chanted in disgust at Mike Jagger's camp strutting gait, suggestive gesticulations, pouting rubber-lipped expressions, and girlish dress. "It'll make men of 'em." People at the Telly tried to get them banned for inciting salaciousness and corruption on our young, impressionable minds. 'Come On', by Chuck Berry, was their first record with Decca, so we liked that, and they followed it up with the raunchy Lennon and McCartney, 'I Wanna Be Your Man'. Then came Bobby Womack's, 'It's All Over Now', then, 'Little Red Rooster', and then they were locked away till they wrote some of their own. The Shadows remained faithful to their image, neat-n-tidy and unaffected by the movement of hair fashion. Cliff Richard has constantly and most successfully (although I'm not so convinced about his West End, Heathcliff bearded bit) changed his hair to create a new image practically every decade. Throughout history, hair has been the focus of change. Another notable 'hair' period was the English Civil War with King Charles I and his ringlet bedecked long cavalier flowing locks, and his deadly opponents in strife, Oliver Cromwell and his pudding basin style Round Heads. There are also the skin heads, and even the most predominant dictator of all, Adolf Hitler and his brushed to one side, slicked down hair style, not to mention that moustache.

THE SANDSTORMS WERE MODISH and during the height of the Mods-n-Rockers' riots which took place along the south coast, I was serving as an indemnified apprentice ladies hair stylist at John Stewart Ladies Hair Fashions in Westover Road, Bournemouth, right opposite the Pavilion Theatre. That was my day job, and whilst The Beatles were performing for a week at the Gaumont Theatre, also in Westover Road, I had the privilege (I felt quite blasé then) whilst at the salon, to see John, Paul, George and Ringo on more than one occasion, casually strolling from their lodgings at the Palace Court Hotel, along the pavement outside. I also enjoyed the dubious pleasure of taking part in the Mods-n-Rockers riots as

a Mod, whilst my workmate, Dave, at the salon was a Rocker. Whilst in the salon, we were both the epitome of obsequiousness and chivalry to the female clients, graciously guiding them to their dressing table chairs, basins and driers. However, once work was over, and following a brief makeover in the staff room, he was transformed into a Rocker, greased back hair an' all, and I had become an instant Mod. Within minutes, we were on opposite sides of The Square in amongst our respective clans (Mods-n-Rockers), violently chasing each other, with the police in close pursuit, down the Exeter Road to the seafront. That's where-n-when the real battle commenced. If piles of deckchairs weren't on fire, they were legitimate ammunition and flying through the air at the enemy (the Rockers) who stood their ground, leather clad, aggressively wielding their vicious looking bicycle chains. I seem to remember that flick knives were around then.

Roger with Gretch guitar

JOHN STEWARTS LADIES HAIR SALON, being situated directly opposite The Pavilion Theatre and Ballroom, meant that we had the opportunity to cater for some of the visiting stars and personalities of the day. I had the good fortune to style the bouffed, flick-up hair of Millicent Martin from the groundbreaking satirical TV show, 'That Was The Week That Was', hosted by David Frost. One of the Kay Sisters was also a client, as well as a Beverley Sister, and some other women who were somebody or something, but being quite young, I wasn't sure who and for what? Whilst titivating their stunning locks, my conceit would overcome me, and I would use the chance to mention that I was playing regularly at The Pavilion as Roger and The Rallies, and The Sandstorms rock group. Just to humour me I'm sure, they would promise that during their interval, they would pop into the ballroom to have a look. I'll never know if they did. Talk's cheap. But if I'm wrong and they did, and I flatter myself that they would remember, I love them all. Another customer to come under the creative stroke of my comb was local entertainer, Connie Creighton. Blonde-n-bubbly, and the consummate pro entertainer, she went on to host the children's puppet show, Sooty and Sweep. Furthermore, Connie was a contemporary of George Fairweather, the gentlemen's hairdresser ..... "Something for the weekend sir?", also of Westover Road. His salon, with the aroma of singed hair, was ensuite to ours (John Stewarts). Early on, and way back when, George and Connie were cabaret-n-stage partners, and lifelong friends of the lad himself, tragic comedian, Tony Hancock.

REHEARSAL SPACE WAS HARD TO FIND but rehearsing was

obviously a great necessity, especially if we were going to get bookings and establish a good reputation on the circuit. It's not commonly known, but there is a vast difference between practice and rehearsal. Practice is something that one does alone, at home, or somewhere away from the world at large. It means individual application, going over and over your material, perhaps to hone in a song, music piece, or the lines of a script until you don't have to think about them. Once, through practice, when things have been mastered, one can then concentrate on the entertainment aspect of the performance and one's rapport with the audience. The boring process of practice is basically number or note crunching. Rehearsal, however, is the final stage. It takes place with the remainder of the cast, dancers or group, and serves to tidy everything up and coordinate with any partners. If people do not use their own time and the obvious effort to practice their parts alone, and then turn up at a rehearsal expecting to put it together at the last minute, the fur will inevitably start to fly, especially if all the others are up to speed and ready to apply their final touches.

AS FAR AS TRANSPORT WAS CONCERNED at the time of The

Sandstorms, none of us were in possession of a suitable vehicle that was capable of carrying all our equipment, PA, drums, amps, instruments, costumes, etc. The convention of driving to gigs and back home late at night, courtesy of a beaten up, draughty and cold, rust bitten old panel van with tons of equipment falling all over us at every bend, somehow just didn't appeal. We'd heard all the weary old war stories of bands slogging around in such miserable, warn-out road wrecks, and many old rock group campaigners, oddly enough, hold that kind of purgatory as some kind of medal of honour. For us, travelling like pop stars (even 'though we weren't) in comfort was our main priority ..... that's where my Father (Charlie) and driver came in again. We all travelled with Charlie as our chauffeur in his blue Morris Oxford car (£850 brand new with blue leather bench seats – very common in cars then and great for getting horizontal for snogging! – and purchased from the Westover Garage in The Square, Bournemouth). Miraculously, all our gear followed behind in a vintage wooden bodied car trailer. It was an amazingly old but durable and gracious chariot, running on two large, wire spoke motorbike wheels, with leaf sprung suspension. It was great – travelling in luxury, style and comfort, and we could have a good laugh (usually about nothing) on the way or on the way home from bookings. As gigs were quite draining with all the setting up, playing, fraternising with fans, breaking all the gear down and loading it back into the transport, we would usually all succumb to sleep on the return journey, leaving Charlie to drive home in the dark with only (no radio then) the accompaniment of the windscreen wipers and us, slumped in a sweaty pile, grunting-n-snoring.

SACKING SANDSTORMS HAPPENED when members of The Sandstorms turned up for rehearsal, not knowing the new numbers. That meant that we couldn't add any dynamics to the piece, and insulted those of the band who had put in the time at home and came prepared. The culprits were not expected to be perfect but reasonably prepared with at least a basic understanding and articulation of a piece. It was as a result of this particular scenario and persistent recurrence that some band members had to be let go (sacked, fired, down-the-road, given the old heave-ho), as it were. Naturally, not knowing one's part wasn't necessarily the whole story. It was usually a combination of contributory factors (the catalyst amongst the pigeons, as the Greek philosopher??? said), leading to an unpleasant and unfortunate dismissal, for instance, personality clashes, unresolved disputes over programme content, plus other day-to-day things that sometimes niggle-n-fester and ultimately erupt. This type of eruption happens often when people with a strong artistic temperament are being creative together. For example, here is a typical incident that caused a rumpus. When we started, we were ninety nine point nine percent non-smokers, and therefore we decided, democratically, and for the comfort of the majority, that the vehicle transporting us to gigs (Charlie's Car) was elected a non-smoking area. A single rider to this regulation was that anyone wishing to travel in Charlie's trailer was free to indulge in the tobacco weed. Later on, this non-smoking regulation blew up into a messy dispute when a good, but boisterous, member of the band decided to blatantly flout our rule, defy us all, including Charlie, and smoke in the car. There was a cataclysmic set-to on one occasion whilst on our way to a gig. Charlie (not being a wilting wallflower when trouble was looming, or one to back out of a dispute), stopped the car and demanded that the culprit refrain from smoking. Stubbornly and most vehemently, the culprit refused Charlie's initial reasoning and all our pleading and subsequent demands to stop, and thus an argument of monumental proportions ensued on the litter encrusted grass verge at the side of the road to a Winchester gig. Thus, this incident, combined with not being up to speed with band material, resulted in an unfortunate 'parting of the waves' as it were.

Of course, this dramatic action sometimes created a little animosity, to say the least, and because of it (giving someone the heave-ho), I became the target for a beating up, and I almost succumbed to a group of youths who had set out, with malice aforethought, to execute such a GBH on my very person. Knowing that I was inside the Pavilion Bournemouth, playing guitar with the Jan Ralfini Orchestra, they had been laying in wait outside, and as I drove away in my car, they aggressively over-took me in an old Colmer van. Suddenly, whilst still moving, the back doors of their van swung open, and three or four of the occupants were hanging out, shouting abusive threats, brandishing weapons and clenched fists. After a few hundred yards, they closed the doors and drove at an intimidating pace ahead of me, swaying from side to side in order to prevent me from passing. They were obviously waiting for a quiet area to block my path, get out and sort me out. Somehow, we arrived at County Gates in Westbourne. (I knew the area well. I'd been chased around that area by a police car late one night for not stopping at a white line. It caught me after I'd turned down a dead-end street. They blocked the entrance with their patrol car, and I received a £10 fine.) With the van still in front of my car, keeping me in check, we approached a side turning that I knew connected with the parallel running, Princess Road. I let them pass it, and then, when almost over it myself, I performed a swift rubber burning right turn into the street. They went straight on. I anticipated that they would turn and follow me, so quickly, I affected a screeching handbrake turn in the street and then waited. As predicted, they came squealing in. My foot was on the floor accelerating, and in milli seconds, I was out onto the main road and made good my escape, leaving them struggling to negotiate a cumbersome old van in a narrow street. Of course, no-one had power steering in those days. They tried it once more as I drove home late at night through Winton. I stopped behind them and waited in my car as they de-bussed and walked angrily towards me. When they were close and quite far from their van, I reversed at speed, turned around using a side street for space, and fled into the dark, tree-lined roads of Red Hill Drive. It never happened again. They'd made their point with youthful male bravado.

The Sandstorms Disc-A-Go-Go

WHAT ABOUT FROFFY COFFEE? Well, even though the rest of the planet was experiencing the first rumbles of a rock-n-roll revolution (here, Tommy Steele was 'Singing the Blues', and a skiffle scene was happening) and the advent of teenagers, coupled with the invention of licentiousness and sex, 'little ole Bournemouth' was still slightly shrouded within its original sedate image. Since the first goatskin-clad, woad painted, club wielding ancient humans straggled down from the plains and came upon the mouth of the River Bourne, put two-n-two together and called it Bournemouth, the locality was always renowned as being a soporific neck of the woods. Back then, it was frequented by hordes of rattling, Victorian-esk bath chairs, and was mainly populated by those with chest and respiratory complaints, and even worse ailments, who had migrated from 'up the smoke', seeking solace and convalescence. Robert Louis Stevenson (famous author, as opposed to this diatribe) was a sickly chap who bought a house in Westbourne, probably because a flashy estate agent, lying through his teeth, pitched him the idea that the location was renowned for its medicinal, healing qualities. The site is still there and marked with a plaque, but not the house as the Germans decided to blow it to smithereens. Admittedly, the town does have a sleepy atmosphere even now, with all its garish night raving clubs, and ranting, highly intoxicated, jolly revellers that play havoc with the Borough's reputation at night.

So, with that background in mind, one can easily comprehend the furore that swept aside the usual local calm when the first 'Coffee Bar' opened in Old Christchurch Road, Bournemouth. "A Coffee Bar, so what?" Nothing out of the ordinary there, you may speculate. Nonetheless, this was different; they were trading 'Frothy Coffee'!! The event was on the front page of all the local newspapers and on the tip of everybody's tongues, and all the kids wanted their parents to take them to this place of 'Frothy Coffee'. "What is it? What's it all about? Where did it come from?" Those were just a few of the irritating questions we kids posed to our Second

World War, weary parents. 'Was this,' they cogitated, 'what they had fought and millions had died for? For 'Frothy Coffee'?' It was those Americans again, they conceded. Not only did they claim to have won the War, single-handed with Audi Murphy, they were now corrupting our good ole ritualistically on doilies 'tea-n-crumpets' cuisine with something called 'Frothy Coffee'. Little did my parents, and many of their generation, realise, and I think, fortunately for them, that they wouldn't live to see the introduction of 'Hamburgers' and the Americanisation of the world. Find the last rain forest tree standing with the last indigenous tribe to be discovered sheltering under it, and inevitably, they'll be wearing base ball caps and trainers. Say no more. Whatever, my parents were both very outgoing and adaptable to the extreme; therefore, it was only a short period of time before the three of us were installed in that devilish 'Frothy Coffee Bar', fidgeting in our seats, eagerly awaiting the experience. The machine that was going to deliver us this delicacy resembled an old-time theatre organ, Reginald Dixon-type (who's he?). The monstrous, percolating vending apparatus, like a feat of engineering that Isambard Kingdom Brunel would have been proud of, and which promised to transport us to new heights of taste and succulence, was a large cube-like, wavy steel structure, the obvious star of the show, and rightly had assumed prime position, centre front of the counter. It had an ornate gold plate corrugated front. There were levers that the girls behind the counter (looking attractive in their obligatory 'American Diner' type outfits) pulled on from time-to-time, and intriguing, shiny chromium-plated pipes woven around its hot, bubbling body. Sudden intermittent purges of steam at jet engine decibel noise levels, created by the abominable apparatus, as it filtered its potion, was amusing and incredible to us. The flavourful aroma permeating our nostrils became tranquilising and sensual. Before the contraption finally ejaculated the, as yet un-tasted, black liquid into smart little glass cups and saucers, it hissed-n-spat like a locomotive preparing to leave the station. The resulting substance was delectable to our baron taste buds, and the milky coffee-coloured froth, that sat fizzing on our smiling top lips, said it all.

More 'pseuds corner' sanctuaries of the jazzy cafe coffee life were dotted liberally around the town. We frequented them, not through thirst, but a need to be seen amongst the lovely people. There was a certain protocol to be followed: one wouldn't just swallow a cup of coffee, pay and disappear refreshed – definitely not! The correct procedure was to sit sipping for, say, three to four hours, or days, feigning a studious, but false, laid backed intellectuality. Smoking was definitely in, as long as it was menthol flavour or Sobranie Black Russian. The Swiss Restaurant, opposite the Upper Gardens, was a popular haunt where Continental students gathered to natter-n-smoke Gitanes. The Hayloft in Yelverton Road, verging on the trendy but more rustic – like an attic playroom – had a bourgeoisie atmosphere with duffle coats, black polo-necked jumpers and the decadent aroma of Woodbines.

The Dynosonic Jerks

REHEARSAL NIGHTS took place in my parent's bungalow. As you can imagine, Rock was in its infancy; we were in our teens, and the neighbours were in their houses trying to get some peace after work. The outcome of that situation was predictable friction. As we turned up the volume, my Father would be confronting the ranting neighbour at the bottom of the garden who was the only one who had an allergy to noisy bands rehearsing. All posthumous praise should go to my Father who, under much duress, displayed an admirable, evangelical attempt to convert our stubborn, agnostic neighbour to the sacred divinity that is Rock-n-Roll. Dad used the convincing hypothesis that, by enduring the rocking, window rattling, rolling racket, it would ultimately benefit society, the nation, and the development of the world as a whole, but, sadly it fell on 'deafened ears'. Unsurprisingly, talks broke down, and respecting his position, his rabid, lead straining dog, and the half brick aimed at our windows, we withdrew to a new location – the wallpaper store room above my uncle's ironmongers' shop. That proved to be just the ticket. No-one lived close by, and therefore we repeated tunes over-n-over until perfection was achieved. Moreover, we could tweak up the volume and go to town, indulging ourselves in an ear blistering, rhythm-n-blues jam session. No particular tune, but just an excuse for some good long, thrashing guitar and drum solos.

We would make sure that we always had all the latest popular hit tunes in our repertoire as soon as they came into the charts, and the record was released and available to us to work on. The only way to learn new numbers in those days was to purchase the 45rpm or 33rpm LP vinyl record, and by repeatedly playing it over and over to become erudite. It kept our list of numbers fresh-n-favourable to the punters who were the important element. As some great performer said, "Never forget, you are only ever fifty percent of any performance. The audience are the other fifty percent and by far the most important percent." The majority of young people didn't want to hear obscure Blues numbers and fancy esoteric material; they just wanted to dance to the latest Beatles and Mersey Beat songs. We obviously had our own personal R&B, Rock, Blues, and Popular instrumental heroes and tastes in music; even so, we had to remember that we were playing for a paying, mainstream audience, and self-indulgence on our part would simply lead to marginalisation of the band, and ultimately, limit venues. Whatever, we totally enjoyed everything we were playing and most of the music of the time, so no problem.

THE MELODY MAKER was probably the world's oldest music newspaper, and it was essential reading for musicians to keep up-to-date with the latest bands, music reviews, the top-ten, and gossip. It also had some very nice pictures.

The flamboyant 'Originator', **BO DIDDLEY,** with his bouncy, trembley rhythmic guitar technique, secured his rightful place in the records of rock history. Bo was a glamorous act, made fun music with titles like 'You Can't Judge A Book', and played some funny, bizarre-shaped, even 'square?', Gretch guitars. I really enjoyed the thrill of playing, 'You Can't Judge A Book By Looking At The Cover'. His stuff, like the song, 'Bo Diddley', in nineteen fifty five, affected Buddy Holly, who produced a magnificent re-penned version called, 'Not Fade Away', and incidentally, it was the last song that he ever sung on that cold wintry night before embarking on his fatal air crash. The Rolling Stones' theatrical, rousing version is another prime example of this particular Bo Diddley rhythm led piece.

With the release of a new Beatles LP, I rushed down to Brights' record shop, Gervis Place, near The Arcade in Bournemouth. Ensconced in one of their soundproof booths, insulated with perforated hardboard that created an entombed 'cotton wool in the ears' atmosphere, I waited with baited breath to hear the Fab Four's latest offering. After a little pause of anticipation, from the speakers, there was the distinctive clump of the stylus being placed onto the spinning vinyl by an unseen shop assistant, and the crackling as it engaged in the record groove. Then came the hiss; my tension heightened, perspiring hands wringing as I listened to the needle dragging through the vinyl furrow closing in on the first track. Suddenly, raising the hairs on the back of my neck, I was blasted with a high energy salvo from the inimitable voice of John Lennon opening their first track ..... "It won't be long, Yea!!!" Ecstasy!

JUKE BOXES were another good source of new material for our repertoire. By listening to what records the punters were playing over-n-over again, we could analyse which were the most popular. These clear plastic domed, ostentatious record blasting beasts, their whirring glitzy bellies gorged with rock singles, were often found where The Sandstorms and girls could be found, namely, transport cafés, parochially pronounced 'caffs'. Girls could also be found in these purveyors of the sausage-n-bacon sarnie, and were vital for more than the obvious because, by listening to what they repeatedly selected on the Juke Box, we had a fair idea of what to include in our list of numbers. Girls pretty much dictated what we played. Cruising at thirty miles an hour in our grey, souped-up Austin 7 banger, we rumbled over the stony, muddy water filled potholes in the café car-park, and ground to a halt. It wasn't a groovy car, and it really didn't do much to impress the chicks. The dames, to whom we were aimed, sitting inside the caff, at their sugar-encrusted, tea-ring stained tables, just laughed through the cracked steamed-up windows, from behind the Tomato and HP Sauce bottles, of the run-down wooden shack of a joint that we, in our infantile minds, thought of as an American Diner. Compared to the leather-clad ton-up blokes, leaning menacingly on their gleaming, chromium plated hot rods, we made no impression. Teds may have had the edge, but our secret weapon, in our bird pulling arsenal, was a simple chat-up line that never failed to work. Initially it took a few froffy coffy's and some spare coins for a few re-plays of her favourite tune to achieve some interest. Then, following some pathetic gems of our vacuous, worldly wit, we would go in for the kill with something along the lines of, "Didn't I see you dancing at The Pavilion last night?" which would usually prompt the reply, "Yea, so where were you?" Straight in with the winning punch-line, "I was up on the stage, playing in the band." Sorted! However suave-n-chunky the male opposition was, it held a lot more kudos than, "Didn't you come into the ironmongers yesterday? I sold you some paraffin. Yea, I know it smells. It's difficult to wash off."

Ticket to Jive

SWERVING SLIGHTLY OFF THE COURSE OF ROCK, I have to say that the café, or greasy spoon, was for some time an essential part of the English gastronomic culture, heritage and cuisine. Gallons of hot, strong, dark brown, tooth-rotting sweet, NAAFI tea was drunk from big chipped battleship earthenware mugs. This was famously accompanied by a gut-lining fried breakfast of monumental proportions. None of your sissy continental croissant and eyeglass of black pitch-like substance called coffee. These pedlars of real food also laid on some scrumptious lunches of Britain ..... bangers-n-mash, roast beef and Yorkshire pud-n-two veg, not forgetting the traditional afters, like yer spotted dick, rhubarb pie, apple pie, gooseberry pie – the same with crumble – all swamped in an illuminous yellow sea of acrylic looking custard. Or there was rice pud with a thick brown skin, brill. Forget drugs, sex-n-booze, a true rock-n-roller's secret yearning is for the café fayre. Relevant fact: I have played guitar duo in a joint not unlike the aforementioned, on several occasions, to the delight of some rather bewildered, breakfast-eating diners. It was a gig – got paid.

As soon as The Beatles first LP, Please Please Me, came out in 1963, I bought it, took it home and sat down to listen-n-learn as many tracks as possible. Once I had them under my belt, with the words on paper and the chords in the correct pattern, I immediately convened a Sandstorms' emergency rehearsal. Unbelievably, through diligence, blistered fingers, sweat and frayed tempers, we managed to learn the complete album and performed it to great effect and audience adulation at The Pavilion Beat Night the very next evening. I still remember Tony's touching renditions of, 'Till There Was You' and 'A Taste Of Honey'.

Dave and I remember that gig with great affection. The ballroom was packed, seething hot-n-smoky with literally thousands packed like sardines. Smoking was allowed everywhere; your eyes wept, and in the morning, our stage costumes were hung out in the garden to freshen up. Dave said that he'd never seen so many people cramped together, except at a football match. He walked to the side entrance and asked the doorman how many were in there. When Dave came back to us in the bar, he told us that the doorman had said there were two thousand five hundred in. At the back of the stage, in full view of the audience, there was a long curved wall, painted matt black, with a small access door right in the centre. It was through that door, in front of two thousand five hundred punters, that we had to make our entrance. Remember, we were nobodies – a young, nervous, wet-behind-the-ears group – but we could play guitar music and were ready for the limelight, however brief the fix. Back stage, none of us spoke; we just paced to-n-fro like caged lions waiting to get at the Christians. The guitars were already in position, sound checked, and plugged in on stands in front of our respective amps. As we walked nervously through the door and clumped down the layered stage in our Cuban heels to pick up our instruments, we were looking into a sea of perspiring heads and expectant faces. The massive main body of people in the centre of the ballroom had pushed forward, squashing several rows of girls at the front edge of the stage so tightly together that their arms were flailing over on to the stage like hundreds of octopus tentacles. Dave later confided that when he sat at the drums in front of this huge throbbing mass, he said he was so frightened that he thought "Sod this, shall I do a runner!" Simultaneously, with Tony and Mike, I snatched my guitar from its stand, flicked the strap over my head, and settled the instrument comfortably into my waist. Turning to face the audience, VOX amp volume at 'WOW', I struck the strings of my Chet Atkins Gretch Country Gent 'Harrison' type guitar with my plectrum. The first dynamic, amplified notes of the familiar intro to 'Twist and Shout' blasted the crammed ballroom. Instantaneously, the audience exploded; girls shook their heads, raised their arms and screamed and went into a wild gyrating frenzy. The screaming was so piercing that our ears (although adapted to loud rock music) were buzzing for hours after. We really felt like rock stars. Legislation dictated that all records must be three and a half minutes long, so for three and a half minutes it was our tune; they were screaming 'literally' at us – a young, eager local band who were enjoying some of the jubilation of Beatles' adulation. We were the first band to play Mersey Beat songs at The Pavilion, and that gig was the talk of the town. Afterwards Dave said, "That's it, we'll go professional, we'll never have to go to work again." Our set was followed by one of our favourite groups, The Sands Combo. They went well but it was different music; the crowd were not so impressed. They were good, but we had given them the taste of something new. The following week, The Sands Combo played some Beatles' songs, but it wasn't the same with sax and organ.

It may have been noticed that, yes, my faithful, gracious Hank Marvin type red Fender Stratocaster guitar had now been replaced by a Chet Atkins Gretch Country Gent, 'Harrison Type'. Why? Because The Beatles had been appearing for one week at the Gaumont Cinema, Westover Road, Bournemouth, and I had been to see them (couldn't hear them for the screaming) twice – once with my parents and once on my own. George Harrison had the Country Gent and so that was the way to go. Compared to the Fender Strat, the Gretch's tone was rather mellow, so to compliment and sharpen it to the new chunky clear Liverpool sound, I bought a VOX thirty watt treble boost amp. The Watkins echo box was also put in mothballs, and I adopted a more distorted sound as was the thing then. To complete our new Beatle-esk, Merseybeat-ish line-up, Tony went out and bought an Epiphone Dreadnought acoustic guitar, like John Lennon's, and Eddie had the proverbial Paul McCartney Hoffner Beatle violin bass guitar.

The Sandstorms, Pavilion, Bournemouth

Not sure how we came to have Eddie on board? He was a tall, thick set chap with an imposing personality, and his family owned a popular local pub that regularly featured bands, and we played some good, rough-n-tumble, beer swilling, nights there. Their inviting hostelry, with a real buxom barmaid pulling pints of delicious real English warm beer, and without a modern, pretentious and overpriced restaurant (they sold crisps), was situated close to a large residential area and therefore attracted a good age range of patrons. Eddie didn't beat-around-the-bush, and if he didn't like you or your opinion, he would let you know. In a tight corner, he was useful to have around. Having said that, he was good spirited, uninhibited fun and fine company. He was not alone as a bit of a Lothario (we were all guilty), and historically, this cocktail of sexual chemicals has often caused distraction and the inevitable upset. Discretion wasn't Eddie's biggest virtue, and there was once, after a public house show in Milford-on-Sea, a feather flying incident, brought about by one of his rather unguarded, suggestive moves towards a member of the band's girlfriend. The girl from the Fan Club and the Sandstorm in question were in the back of Charlie's car, engaging in some physical hot stuff. Without warning, Eddie thrust himself in through the door and bounced down heavily on the back seat besides them. Brazenly, even though she was in the clutches of another chap, Eddie flung his arm around her shoulder and suggested that if she played her cards right (or words to that effect), she could experience his experience, and experience a much better time with him. In a few seconds, rival male blood rose to boiling, and then the two stags locked antlers in an eruption of malevolence. Both grappling bodies fell out through the vehicle door and thumped, audibly, onto the gravel car park. For a few moments in the gloom of the poorly illuminated pub park, with the girl trying to drag them apart, they sprawled, all gangling legs-n-elbows, wrestling with each other in the dirt-n-fag ends. Tony and I were loading the gear into the trailer, and in seconds, we were pulling the opponents apart and back onto their unsteady feet. Spitting dust, and staring defiantly at each other, they quickly calmed down. Dishevelled, they straightened their ties, tucked in their shirts, and reluctantly, trying to look groovy and un-humiliated, the ex-competitors mucked in to get the rest of the amps and PA stowed. By the time we left the venue, there was no question of animosity, it was sorted, and we all laughed and made friendly jibes on the journey home. I have to admit, rather admiringly, that Eddie's lack of subtlety on that occasion worked because, as they say in Westerns, 'He got the gal'.

Similarly, to complete the change, Dave updated his kit to a swish new set of Rogers drums. Dave and I had been to a Friday night drum demonstration at Minns Music shop in Gervis Place, featuring Kenny Clare, the wizard percussionist from the Jack Parnell band. During that insecure, self-conscious, affected period of life, we never wore more clothes than was completely necessary. Even in adverse weather conditions, we wouldn't heed the nagging parental advice to, 'wrap-up warm-n-dry', because it just didn't look funky. Roads had flooded locally that day, and on the telly news, rowing-boats full of firemen (that's what they were called then, because they put fires out, not fought with them) were floating up the high street, rescuing demented scruffy pets, and old people wearing check zip-up slippers and stupid plastic head scarves. Consequently, two drowned rats squelched into Minns Music shop that evening. Sitting down in a pool of water, I vividly remember reaching into my sodden, skin-tight trousers pocket to find my plectrum (thought I might have a strum on a couple of guitars), and instead, felt a piece of wet, pathetic pulped papier-mâché at the bottom which had once been my return bus ticket home. I availed myself, and Dave, of some complimentary canapés (vol-aux-vents and cheesy things on wooden tooth-picks) that had been spread on a white table cloth draped over the shop counter, along with half a dozen free brochures, and several dozen mind-quenching schooners of cheap sherry. Once Dave had clapped his rhythmic drummer's eyes on that Rogers kit that Kenny was going ballistic on, it was a definite, must have. Just one obstacle – his parents.

Initially, his mother had said, "Definitely not!" After a bit of deliberation, Dave decided that a confrontation was necessary and so went to his mother with an ultimatum. "Either I'm going to become a greaser, and hang around on street corners with a bicycle chain, or a drummer; it's up to you." Her reaction was to go straight round to see my Mother. After a brief, ten-to-the-dozen matriarchal con-flab, she agreed that he should go straight out and buy the drums as it would keep him off the streets. Dutifully, a flunky driver in a Minns Music shop small Morris delivery van delivered the spanking new drum-kit at the door of the Hitchings' bungalow. It cost 253 quid. Doesn't seem much now, but we have to remember that the average man's wage in the sixties was a pitiful £17.10 shillings a week, and he probably had an outside toilet. Therefore, Dave's new drums represented 14 weeks', hard grafted for, wages. Converted to today's money, it would be about £7,700. What Dave didn't realise was that the mothers had decided that all the new equipment, Dave's Rogers drums and my Gretch guitar, would be paid for from our gig money. It took quite a lot of gigs to pay back the 300 guineas that my Gretch cost. I was earning £2.10 shillings a week as an apprentice hairstylist, and Dave was pulling in a princely 10 (old) pence an hour, slogging on a lathe in a pit of metal shavings for forty four hours a week as an apprentice engineer.

Club Rio

In the beginning, there were **INSTRUMENTALS**, and the world was instrumentals, and nothing but instrumentals, and so it was with The Sandstorms' repertoire. It came to be because I was inspired by the aforementioned, 'Peter Gun' from the remarkable twangy guitar of Duane Eddy, and the aid of Bert Weedon's book, 'Play in a Day'. Studying his book, I learnt three chords and how to tune-up. Apparently, John Lennon and Paul McCartney learnt A and E from his book! I obviously learnt the wrong chords! After that, it was The Ventures of America who gave me my next piece, 'Walk Don't Run'. It made me feel that I was playing the guitar for real. 'Walk Don't Run' was relatively easy, but it had a dynamic intro with easy powerful chords, and a memorable, simple tune. Next, along came The Shadows with 'F.B.I.' That tune still evokes the same adrenalin rush that I experienced the very first time that I heard it. Anachronistic I know, but it takes all tastes to make a world, and for me, it's one of those tunes that conjures up a time, place, and even a smell and taste.

There were loads of instrumental groups in the early days, and I was very sad when we had to hone the instrumentals down and take on vocals. The Sandstorms' instrumental period was one of my favourite chapters and I sadly mourn its loss, and envy Hank Marvin who was blessed with a life and a permanent audience to hear him playing those amazing tunes. The Ventures of America was probably the first major, influential, and long running instrumental band. 'Walk Don't Run' was The Ventures first tune, but nobody wanted it. Taking things into her own hands, one of the group's mothers recorded it on her own label. It was then picked up by a major company and eventually reached number two in The States. Other groups that we emulated by using their tunes were, Surfers (Wipe Out), Pyramids (Pipeline), The Shadows, The Spotnicks, The Crew Cats, The Tornados, Johnny and the Hurricanes (Sandstorm – derivation of The Sandstorms), and don't forget the twangy guitar of the one-n-only, Duane Eddy.

THE LIST OF NUMBERS was very important. It meant the difference between success and failure to please our audience, and whether or not we would appeal to their discerning taste in popular music, and our ability to satisfy their insatiable appetite for all the current hits.

Do Ya Wanna Dance and Too Late Now **ARE A SAMPLE LIST OF VOCALS FROM OUR REPERTOIRE ALONG WITH** From Me To You. Put On Your Dancing Shoes. I'm Looking For Someone To Love. Come On. Thank You Girl. Boys. Some Other Guy. Too Much Monkey Business. I Wanna Be Your Man. A Rock N Roll Nurse. No Particular Place To Go. If You Gotta Make A Fool Of Somebody. Money. By The Way. Just Like Me. There's A Place. The Shake. Do You Love Me? Roll Over Beethoven. Here's Hoping. Where Have All The Flowers Gone? From Me To You. Our Rendezvous. See If She Cares. I Like It. Hard Days Night. The Fortune Teller. A Shot Of Rhythm And Blues. The Huly Guly. Twist And Shout. Zip A Dee Doo Dah. Then I've Got Everything. Memphis Tennessee. The Twamp. Bo Diddley. High Heel Sneakers. I'm Telling You Now. Love Potion No. 9. A Taste Of Honey. Reelin And Rockin. I'll Keep You Satisfied. Sugar And Spice. Misery. She Loves You. Green Green. Maybelline. Johnny B Goode. Amapola. I'm Telling You Now. Till There Was You. I'll Get You. Bad To Me. That's What I Want. Ain't Gonna Kiss Ya. It's So Easy. Thirty Days. Move It. Please Please Me. Jenny Jenny. Long Tall Sally.

And some of our Instrumentals were: Shaddoogie. F.B.I. Nivram. Joe's Song. Twisted. Dance On. Come September. Trambone. Walk Don't Run. Man Of Mystery. The Stranger. Guitar Boogie. Apache. Wipe Out. Moon Shot. Shazam. The Cruel Sea. Happy Hendricks Polka. Hava Nagila. Perfidia. Jacks Good. Wonderful Land. Guitar Twist. Foot Tapper. Pipe Line. In The Hall Of The Mountain King.

BILL AND ANN LEGGE were well-known, well-established and respected local dance teachers. They ran a stylish dance studio above a shop in Winton, Bournemouth. Being experts in their field and always creative in their endeavours to encourage customers to their studio, they decided, in their infinite wisdom, to engage the services of The Sandstorms. Rock groups had become prevalent and popular, and they were going to exploit it to their benefit, and so a 'Twist-n-Jive' night was arranged. Tickets were printed, requesting suits-n-ties to be worn, and in just a few hours, were sold out. Obviously, the venue was limited space wise, but Bill and Ann achieved their goal. We set-up and performed at one end of the wooden dance floor. Being a dance studio, it was a bit bland and clinical and the stark strip lighting overhead drained the room and everyone in it of all colour. This bland situation was quickly resolved when Bill and Ann created a circle in the midst of the dancers, and proceeded with the promised, 'Twist-n-Jive' demonstration. First, Bill stood in the centre of the circle, and presented a confident, frantic, robust and extremely sincere, but regimented, Twist demonstration. Wringing his wiry body up-n-down like a drill bit to The Sandstorms' version of, 'Let's Twist Again', his knobbly knees bowed in-n-out like spokes of an umbrella opening and closing. Ann was next, centre floor, with her pedantic, 'Come Dancing' Jive lesson. They certainly put the colour back into the room, and everyone twisted and jived the night away ..... well, till ten thirty. Everyone left quietly so as not to wake the slumbering neighbours, some clutching spot prizes like crockery, an eiderdown or a huge teddy bear. That night The Sandstorms had introduced two new songs from the Hit Parade which, to Dave's delight, included the use of his new percussion instrument, the cow bell. 'You Can't Do That' ("My best composition," John Lennon) featured a prominent cow bell, and Dave went to town on it. It gave the tune drive, and we were to use it in the future with great effect in other Beatles' songs, and Rolling Stones' numbers like 'Honky Tonk Woman'. Dean previewed his version of Billy J Kramer's 'Little Children' but I wasn't impressed, not because of his delivery – it was requested twice more – I just didn't like the song. But to be contrary, with the passing of many years, I do now (quite), like it.

LIKE CLIFF RICHARD HIMSELF, and as a Cliff-a-like, Dean Fane endured a bit of ridicule from some of the more rowdy elements in the crowd at some gigs. There was one song in particular that always came in for some serious ribbing from certain parts of the audience. Naturally, it was a Cliff Richard and The Shadows' number – called, 'I Cannot Find a True Love' (from the LP Me and My Shadows) – and it started off with Dean, microphone clutched between both hands, crooning a slow, pathetic solo introduction of pleading, lamentable lost-love. "Where, oh where" ..... slight pause and a few lonely, bluesy notes on guitar ..... "can a true love be?" ..... another pause and a little ripple from Dave on the drums. Any self-respecting thugs at the bar would now be getting agitated with this sentimental claptrap. Not very sophisticated, sarcastic heckles would be bawled out like, "Get on with it Cliff," followed by roars of laughter around the venue. Unperturbed, still moving like Cliff, and being Cliff to the last drop, Dean would carry on relentless, treating them with the contempt he thought they all deserved. "Is she here in London?" ..... definitely juice for more heckles. "No," they continued to taunt. "She's down here with me at the bar, and I'm taking her back to my place later, sorry Cliff." More roars from the crowd. To everybody's relief in the band, and before any of the gang of macho blokes could take it into their heads to impress the girls by dragging our Cliff-a-like off the stage and giving him a serious beating, Dean would finally get to the gravy. Our delicate necks were saved from the rough-necks when our instruments kicked in with a driving rock rhythm and Dean gave it a raucous, "Or in Memphis Tennessee?", and we were off on a fast rollercoaster rocker. In no way am I being unkind to Dean, who was a confident melodic singer, but a soulful intro like that, in the right skilful hands of a star, or even Cliff Richard himself, in a packed auditorium, would be certain to evoke a sympathetic reaction to the emotion of the piece. But sadly, and hilariously for us behind him in the band, given to Dean, our Cliff-a-like, there was no quarter given. Those lonesome lovelorn words were lost on the likes of the unsophisticated at the bar. His sad request for his unrequited love to come on back to him fell on unsympathetic ears. On the contrary, it just got them rattled; it was like bait to a piranha fish, or a red rag to a bull. Hackles were up, and our smart suited Cliff-a-like was fair game for the lads. It may sound a bit insincere, but we quite enjoyed that part of the evening, even 'though it was at our poor vocalist's expense. The reaction was always so predictable, and we could snigger away, cowardly in the background, whilst our always confident, Cliff-a-like, took the brick bats.

Not only did our instruments change due to the new Mersey Beat influences, our clothes (we even wore a set of black-n-white spotted shirts that made us look like the 'One hundred and one Dalmatians') and the line-up had made a dramatic alteration. Eddie was now on bass (someone said that he used to work for a pawn-brokers shop. Or was it a porn shop?), and Dean Fane, our Cliff sing-alike, had been given the elbow. Reflecting our youthful audacity, we held on to Dean's PA system and continued to use it. Dean's dad was not amused by that arrangement (although it did seem to the majority to be democratic), and predictably turned up at the 45 Club, noticeably seething with pent-up rage, looking vengeful, and determined to retrieve the said item. We had been playing for about half an hour when, from the stage, we spotted Dean's father at the door. Following a brief contretemps with the management (Charlie), fingers prodding chests, cigar butts thrown down, he strode, determinedly, through the crowd, like Holy Moses parting the Red Sea, towards us on the stage. Seemingly oblivious, but more than probably choosing to ignore the fact that we were still up there playing, he began to furiously dismantle the PA system. Having been seriously unplugged in the vocal area, we stubbornly continued to play, but with dead mikes, we looked like a mime act. Eventually we gave in and decided to mouth an instant break. During the interval, with Dean, quiet and looking a bit sheepish, and his dad throwing withering comments about us being no better than common thieves, they removed their equipment, and we played the rest of the night using our guitar amps for vocals. What a laugh, eh? You couldn't make it up, could you!?

The Sandstorms with girl duo

GIRLS-N-FANS were never in short supply on the Bournemouth club beat scene, and like any young bloke in a rock band – big, medium or small time – and no matter what one looked like – very attractive, good looking, fair or with a certain degree of character (as they call ugly people in the acting fraternity) – one could date every morning, noon and night, if you had the inclination and the energy. Group or no group, as youngsters, dating wasn't the problem; the real problem was where to go without a car. There were the dark dank golf links or parks, or if you were fortunate to have a car, there were plenty of solitary car parks for hanky-panky. Failing all that, there was the back row of the flicks. Bournemouth also had, and still has, a large intake of foreign students who frequented the various beat venues. Not only that, but a great proportion of them were female. I have to confess that my loyalty and faith was with my music, and to a large extent that always came first, but that doesn't diminish the fact that in the Wild West of Dorset (though it was Hampshire then), a man's gotta do, what a man's gotta do, and so we did!

Once, unbelievably, after one of our frequent gigs at The Crown, Milford-on-Sea, and characteristically exhibiting mischievous innocent youthful male bravado and nothing more sinister or salacious, we managed to smuggle a girl (a fully paid up member of our Fan Club and willing participant in our conspiracy) back home (via the floor of Charlie's car) to my parents' bungalow, where we hid her in my bedroom wardrobe! Curious, and you may well ask, "How did this situation come about? What happened, and how did we get away with it?" It came about because of a particular post gig routine that we followed. Subsequent to a distant booking (we covered a wide radius), and if we were late getting back, plus considering the fact that we also had to unload all the equipment, the post gig arrangement was implemented, i.e.: Dave lived nearby and therefore would go home. Tony and Dean however, lived much further away, and so it was more practical for them to stay overnight in my room. In the morning (following a plate of my mother's bacon, egg, fried bread, mushrooms, beans, toast and marmalade), my Father would take Tony and Dean home to their respective homes. This was early on in our band days, and we were all young and a bit naive and innocent with regard to the opposite sex. The newspaper stated, 'The youngest member of The Sandstorms Beat Group is just fourteen!' Obviously, that didn't mean that we didn't have all the working parts, plus the natural chemically induced inclination, but in those days, there was a lot of what was termed, snogging, and a hand slipping towards the wrong place would prompt a stinging slap. But back to the girl fan in my bedroom wardrobe. Even though there was a lot of laughing at our cheeky jape (throughout what was left of the night), she never came out of the wardrobe until the morning. However, that wasn't the end of it. Just as she jumped out of my bedroom window and ran off down the road, there was serious knocking on the front door by a police officer accompanied by the girl's irate father. I remained in the bedroom with Tony and Dean listening to the rumpus until they came to search the bedroom. Obviously, they found nothing there, and left satisfied that we were totally innocent. We never admitted that she had been there to anyone, but we discovered why the police and her father had come round. Apparently, they had gone to Dave's house first, and he had told them that she was at my house. Grass! Later we discovered that when the girl arrived home, she had wily concocted a good excuse for her late arrival, and fortunately all was ok.

IT'S A BUBBLE-N-SQUEAK WORLD AND GIGS AND TRAVEL WAS HUNGRY WORK

and when we arrived home, we were all ready, mouths salivating, for a good hot sizzling fry-up! More often than not, there was a fantastic all night café somewhere on the side of the road home. We'd be in there, leaving the Morris Oxford and trailer full of amps-n-kit, standing in the rough potholed gravel car park, clicking-n-groaning as the hot engine metal cooled down in the cool night. Chipped mugs of steaming tea and the proverbial fry-up were noshed in ritualistic silence. If, however, we didn't encounter a café, then Charlie was a dab hand and undisputed king of the fry-up ..... egg, bacon, baked beans, mushrooms, fried bread, sausage, black pudding, toast and marmalade, not forgetting the one most important ingredient of all, 'Bubble-n-Squeak'. Personally, I don't think Bubble-n-Squeak receives the amount of adulation that it truly deserves. In fact, there should be legislation requiring that everyone eat at least one helping a day. I can't conceive that there is anyone who doesn't love Bubble-n-Squeak, all washed down with copious amounts of hot strong tea. For those new to the world of Bubble-n-Squeak and its main constituents, the deal is: leftover vegetables from the Sunday roast beef and Yorkshire pudding, but traditionally, it should consist of leftover boiled potatoes-n-cabbage, fried in the frying pan, and cooked at high temperature like a giant pancake. Turn the pat over very occasionally, but make sure that each side is well browned off (can be a bit burnt if you wish), and then tip it onto a warm plate and serve with lashings of Branston Pickle. It is acceptable to add leftover carrots, peas, onions, Brussel sprouts and even old soggy roast potatoes. Just don't get too precious about it, enjoy it. Warning: the kitchen gets a bit smoked up if you leave it cooking to have a brief strum on your guitar and lose all track of time, so make sure that you put the battery back in the fire alarm from when you burnt the toast. Perhaps a fire blanket and a small domestic extinguisher would be a good precaution. While we're on the subject, what happened to faggots-n-peas? (Not the double act, but another dish of the English staple diet.)

Almost without exception, the local clubs and dives, in an antiquated way, as an incentive to draw people in, offered the luxury of 'Scampi in the Basket'. Believe me, this was a big deal back then.

THE SANDSTORMS' RECORDING SESSION took place at the Wessex Recording Studio in Yelverton Road, Bournemouth, and it was great fun-n-frolics. We had a whole bunch of our own songs – good, bad and indifferent (that's not a title) – in quality, and 'Take It From Me', a vocal, was the name of the 45 rpm record that we decided to cut, and on the reverse side was another song, 'The Raider', an instrumental. It was released on a local label, the name of which escapes me. It didn't have a distributor, or any advertising budget behind it. It wasn't promoted much further than the county limits, and consequently, it went nowhere. I know it had some potential, and was as good as some of the stuff that was being churned out at the time, but we just didn't have the influential contacts. Locally, we knew some of the 'right people'; they liked what we did, and could get us some nice gigs in and around, but we lacked the far reaching contacts

necessary to be effective on the national or international market. Not only that, I don't even have a copy. So, if anyone has one, I would be most grateful to have it, or to make a copy.

A particularly memorable occasion when **DAVE AND ROGER MET THE SHADOWS AND SPARRED WITH HANK MARVIN** was during a visit to see The Shadows in concert at the Winter Gardens theatre in Bournemouth. We both took our seats in the centre of the front row and sat sucking Kiora orange juice from grease-proof cardboard cartons, through straws, waiting with excited anticipation for Hank Marvin, Bruce Welsh, Tony Mean and Jet Harris, collectively known as The Shadows. At the beginning of the show, the theatre went dark, and I remember vividly seeing them sneaking onto the stage in the gloom. They stood still, shadowy human shapes with their backs to the audience, causing a moment's anticipation. Suddenly, the stage lights went up, and Hank Marvin, whilst playing the dynamic opening notes of 'Shasam' (by Duane Eddy), swung round to face us, his trade mark red Fender Stratocaster guitar gleaming in the beams of hundreds of spotlights. At certain times in the piece, the other musicians turned, and the hairs on our necks stood in honour of our heroes.

Encore done, audience still roaring for more, The Shadows headed for the wings. The Sandstorms had performed on that very stage many times, and we knew the lay out and that in a few seconds Hank would be in the wings and down the steps to his dressing room. Harbouring this vital geographic knowledge, Dave and I arrived at the side of the stage even before Hank, and we were through the door and blocking the bottom of the stage exit steps. Subsequently, we found ourselves in the envious position of standing with Hank Marvin. He was real, breathing and sweaty. The Fender was also sweaty. He politely conversed with us, but being fan dumbstruck, I remember nothing. He probably asked if we had enjoyed the show and we probably made some inane, puerile spluttering. I noticed that he was still holding his plectrum between his thumb and index finger. I asked if I could have it. He said "Yes", and both of us lunged at him, putting him off balance. "Ok! Ok!" Hank retorted, desperately trying to stay upright, "Hang on, patience, I've got another one here – you can both have one," whereupon, he produced an identical plectrum from his pocket, and we both went away satisfied with a souvenir each. For some time afterwards, we wore the plectrums around our respective necks on pieces of brown parcel wrapping string. Sad gits. I still have many of The Shadows' EP's, LP's and singles on original vinyl.

The Shadows are still heroes of mine, and even today at the time of writing, I hold a great affection for the music that they have given guitarists like me. All their music is still as fresh to me as it was the first time I ever heard it. They gave me something I could reach and was possible to emulate on my own beautiful, sensuous Red Fender guitar. Additional trips to the Winter Gardens proved fruitful, introducing us to a blind artist (who was guided to the centre stage mike by a minder) and future star – Stevie Wonder. Another time, we saw the influential guitarist, Carl Perkins (who penned amongst others 'Blue Suede Shoes') with King Sized Taylor backing. Having purchased first house tickets, and on our way to a gig in Southampton, The Sandstorms saw Chuck Berry. Prior to Chuck's spot, another unknown to us at the time – Eric Burdon of The Animals – finished his set with a blazing version of 'The House of The Rising Sun'.

THE BIG THREE from Liverpool were a favourite group of ours. 'Some Other Guy', their brilliant, sap rising, rhythm led song, was always in our repertoire. For us, it was a feel good song with attack, and manly to perform. Rory Storm and The Hurricanes, 'By The Way', was another in the same vein.

'**NIVRAM**' (Marvin, as in Hank, backwards), by The Shadows, had a splendid bass solo, originally recorded by Jet Harris. Having mastered the lead part, Mike and I spent a happy evening together, applying ourselves to the task of working out his bass line and solo. We incorporated a method of learning the bass that I had stolen from my cousin Colin, who played bass guitar in a band from Portsmouth. We would speed the 45 record up to 78 rpm, which had the effect of making the bass line more prominent. Between short bouts of learning the part, we stopped for the occasional tea break and a general chin wag. Out of the blue, whilst dunking his digestive biscuit, and not even looking up, Mike asked me if I knew what 'French Kissing' was. This sounds sexual, I thought, and I ought to know. After a couple of seconds, and feeling rather humiliated, I had to confess that I didn't. Mike, affecting a superior manner, and pretending to be erudite in all things sexual, went onto explain to me that 'French Kissing' involved the sticking of one's tongue into someone-else's mouth whilst kissing (obviously somebody that wants to be kissing you in the first place). I'd also dunked my digestive biscuit, and as if on cue, and as though the biscuit was shocked by Mike's revelation, the damp bit fell back into my tea, with a plop. I couldn't wait to try it out ….. the kissing, not the biscuit. Unfortunately, Mike had a date coming up the next night, before me, and was taking his girlfriend to the pictures. We agreed, with a ceremonial handshake, that while they were in the back row kissing, he would thrust his tongue in her mouth and monitor the reaction. I made him promise, through pain of being dismissed from the group, to tell me in graphic detail what had happened. The only pitfall that we could think of was, "What if she bites your tongue off?" This anecdote will seem very naïve and ill-informed to children now, but kids were very innocent and sexually unaware then, and remember, at the beginning of The Sandstorms, our youngest member was only fourteen. Be gentle. I realise that these kinds of instrumentals (of which I was talking, before ruminating about 'French Kissing') are not to everyone's taste, but for us, they were great to play, and furthermore, what's the point of playing music that you don't enjoy? Fortunately for us, we enjoyed everything in our list of numbers. I think that during a three hour gig, we were entitled to a bit of self-indulgence, don't you?

WITH REGARD TO EQUIPMENT, A DECENT P.A along with guitar amplification for a rock band is obviously an essential commodity, but when we started, the real good named kit, i.e. Vox, Fender, Marshall, wasn't easy to come by or afford. Today there are millions of music shops dealing with every kind of instrument, effect and amplifier. The embryonic stage of The Sandstorms (with regard to guitar amps and PA systems) saw us kicking off with discarded valve wireless sets and speakers scrounged for pennies from second-hand radio equipment shops. All members of the group were extremely adept at wiring things up and soldering. In fact, we always had a small suitcase full of spare electrical components, screwdrivers, wire cutters, plus, of course, the essential soldering iron and flux. It acquired the nickname, 'The box of tricks'. The box of tricks contained millions of electrical items that had been cannibalised at some time. There were numerous shapes and sizes and kinds of Bakelite plugs. Most of the plugs had the top panel or one or more of its brass pegs missing, but they never got thrown out because, of course, "You never know when it might come in useful, do you?" Odd lengths of mains cable, with the red, green and black integral wires, were coiled up and chucked in the mix, with scores of broken jack plugs, and old microphone carcasses with the gauze dome missing, exposing the thin integral wires dangling from the end of the body.

Seemingly, and incredulous to modern generations (who now passively accept the stifling, oppressive, authoritarian and institutionalised government legislations blighting our once free-n-glorious country), there was a time before the current hounding by the petit bureaucracy of Health and Safety. Many of the venues' so-called 'wiring systems' were practically lethal to anything that had life. Artists in bands did die from electrocution. Occasionally we heard news that someone had been electrocuted at a gig by touching the mike with their lips or fingers on guitar strings. Even so, we were all very pragmatic and never considered the risk of death by electrocution. It was something that happened in America, in a specially designed 'chair'. It was almost expected that whilst singing or strumming a guitar at a gig, one would occasionally, or more likely, always receive a small 'poke', or tingly electric shock, from an unprotected current, particularly when rockin' hot-n-sweaty. The size and design of electric sockets at venues such as village halls, varied so much that we always made sure that we had a good supply of matchsticks with us. If the holes in the socket didn't match the three pinned plug on our extension lead, we would take the plug off, and dextrously (so as not to touch the live bits and be blown to kingdom-come) stick the bare cable wires into the holes of the socket. They would then be secured by poking a match (with the incendiary tip removed in case of fire), or a couple of matchsticks, in as a wedge. Unbelievably, sometimes there wasn't an earth and therefore only accommodation for two wires. Eventually, we came across a universal plug with a host of pegs that would, ostensibly, fit any permutation of mains power system, even in the most rustic scout hut. The earlier models weren't very successful, and the pegs would either fall out, or push back into the body, and no amount of poking with a screwdriver would entice them out. It all sounds very primitive and rather prehistoric and yes, it certainly was, but we were all extremely creative because you had to be. It seems strange now, but you couldn't just drive off to some huge shopping area or industrial estate because they didn't exist.

It was the same scenario for instruments. At first they were very difficult to get hold of, especially the American variety. A line-up on stage of the latest kit, i.e. VOX, Marshall or Fender amps with matching Fender guitars, was, and still is, an important cosmetic, as well as functional, factor. This lack of equipment outlets and shortage of money during that era only served to stimulate our pragmatic intellect, resourceful ingenuity and creativity. Tony and I had two splendid thirty watt VOX amps, but unfortunately, our bass player, Mike, had a small Marshall amp (not in a box) with a separate speaker cabinet on coffee table legs. For the band to achieve an impressive line-up of VOX amps on stage, and to boost the aesthetic, entertainment aspect, we decided to build our own 'look alike' VOX cabinet with Mike's bass amp and speaker secreted subtly inside. My Father and I retired to his workshop and made the wooden cabinet to the exact proportions of the real one. Dave produced a roll of the authentic black PVC material from the craft shop, along with some thin gold plastic piping, to be glued on the outside. My Mother, with her bare nimble fingers, thimble-n-thread, set about the long laborious, eye straining task of sewing the distinctive criss-cross pattern design, identical to the front cover of a real VOX amp. Using a hacksaw, file, vice, and a lot of elbow grease, we managed to fashion a one quarter inch thick solid square of brass into a very convincing VOX insignia. Finally, with the addition of three plastic handles and authentic vents, we had our matching line-up. What steadfast devotion!

EVENTUALLY THE SHADOWS' WALK WAS PUSHED ASIDE

in favour of The Beatles' pose. From Hank Marvin's low slung guitar look and banana-shaped stance, rock musicians' instruments suddenly crawled up, imitating Lennon and Harrison, to chest height, just short of the chin. This new guitar position also incorporated a different posture. Out went The Shadows Walk and in came the frogs legs look. Whilst strumming the guitar across the chest, the artist would bounce up-n-down slightly, knees pointing outwards with the legs bowing and slightly flexing. Another important innovation was the inimitable, Beatles head shake. At certain intervals, we would shake our heads, hair flailing like mops. Pathetic, but visually effective.

The Sandstorms

THE SONG 'DO YOU LOVE ME?' is yet another musical gem in our affectionate memories. Our version was religiously copied, note for note, from Brian Poole and The Tremeloes' recording on Polydore, and retained all the vital dynamics needed to send our band and the dancers completely berserk. There were powerful stops, and rising harmonies. If you know it, you'll recognise the, ah, aah, aaah aaaah, yeahhh, whaaay, "Watch me now, push, push, shake it up, shake it up"...etc. Great stuff, eh? Yeah! Well you had to be there.

STAGE COSTUMES AND POPULAR GROUPS dramatically influenced public dress and the fashion industry with groups during the fifties and sixties being very conscious of their image, and that was reflected in their attention to detail with regard to their dress. At the beginning, smart suits with accessories, like crepes (shoes, not French pancakes, but I wouldn't say no to a crepe suzette) or winkle picker shoes with fluorescent socks were the order of the day, influenced by the likes of The Shadows, Cliff Richard and even Elvis. As a teenager, I remember longing to have some winkle pickers. Similar to most parents of that era, my Mother was adamant that I would only be seen in them over her dead body. The actual process of murder, plus what form it would take, passed through my mind for some days, but it was always stifled by the thought of languishing in jail, plus the overwhelming worry that I wasn't sure, or able to establish, if capital punishment had been abolished in England. Murder no longer an option, but remaining a precocious, stubborn teenager to the last, I rummaged through my bedroom drawers and trousers, gathered up my meagre pocket money, topped it up by scrounging from my aunt and uncle, and trolleybused off to a well-known winkle picker shoe shop in Moordown, Bournemouth. (Yes, there were beautiful environmentally friendly trolleybuses back then. When changing direction, the conductor would get out, and with a long pole, would move the antennae to another wire. There was also a turntable in Christchurch High Street that served to point the bus back in its return direction. Wonderful days!) With glee, adrenalin flowing like an arch criminal perpetrating the crime of the century, I bought the sharpest pair of black Denson High Pointers. For weeks they remained hidden at the back of my wardrobe, smuggled out on occasions to be worn at liaisons with my friends. Of course, like most mothers with their infuriating woman's intuition, she probably knew all the time. Eventually, one day, whilst sneaking out of the house, winklers stuffed up my jumper like a ferret smuggler, she stopped me at the front door with a wry, knowing smile saying, "Look, if you're that determined to ruin your feet for life (prophetically, it did), you might as well put them on before you leave home."

Even The Beatles started off wearing their distinctive uniform, smart Germanic jackets, narrow trousers and Cuban heeled boots. We followed suit (excuse the pun) and had matching suits made so that we resembled The Shadows. I have to confess that I even wore a pair of black horn-rimmed glasses, just like Hank Marvin, except that mine didn't have any glass in them. They also made me look like Buddy Holly, but not so tall or curly haired or as famous. With the advent of The Beatles, we had new suits, but to be marginally original, we had jackets with lower cut collars, and dutifully ordered our Beatles Cuban heeled boots from a supplier in London. Music-n-fashion was evolving and changing by the day. Endless new bands appeared, almost daily, all hailing, some rather dubiously, from

Liverpool. Some would have one or two good hits, then drift along for a while and eventually into obscurity. We used to put on a Liverpool accent to impress the girls in the audience, but we couldn't keep it up, and would eventually slip back to our own Bournemouth brogue. Major groups which produced a regular flow of new material thrived and became bigger, richer and higher, and their clothes became more creative and lurid. Trends didn't slip the notice of The Sandstorms. On stage we were vagabonds ..... tight trousers, thick buckled leather belts, waistcoats, open necked high collared shirts, but we still wore the Chucka Beatle Boots.

The Sandstorms, 45 Club

SOME OTHER BANDS that we had the great pleasure to work with were,
The Bunch, Tony and Howard with The Dictators, The Traitors, The Transatlantics, The Ragtimers, The Kentucky Jazz Band, Mike Allard and The Tremors, The King Pins, Mark and The Sapphires, The Chevrons, The ST Three, The Corvettes, The Wisemen, The Tallmen, The Dominators, Lynn Star and The Saturns, The Inner Circle, Freebooters, Trackmarks, Blackjacks, The Puppets, The Johnny Quantrose 5, The Bobby Bure Group, Howard Tilly Group, The Rabble, Freewheelers, The Conquerors, Fourunners, Steve Marriot (Small Faces) and The Magic Moments, The Hustlers, The Initials Beat Combo, Barry and The Blue Stars, Dave and The Concords, The Barbarians, The South Coast Five, Lee Person and The Defenders, Bob and The KDC, Mundane, The Whackers, Shane and The Shane Gang, The Byrds, Sir Tain and The Certs, Paul Newman and the Surfin Gremmies, Tony Blackburn and the Rovers, The

Planets, Eddie Drake with The Salvoes, The Impacts, Lisa and The Brethren, 4 Teens, Ricky Vernon, The Pathfinders, Johnny Royal and The Hawks, Paul Dean and The Thoughts, Paul Dean and The Gaylords (Marmalade), The Profile, Russ Sainty and The New Notes, Davie Jones (David Bowie) and The Lower Third, Jacqueline Rivers and The Boyfriends, The Denisons, The Size Seven, Bob and the KDC, The Del Rio Five, Lee Peterson and The Defenders. It's amazing that there were so many local bands around then, so it was a great privilege for The Sandstorms to be engaged on a regular basis at The Pavilion and other such grand venues. Having said that, we felt fine at all our gigs, big or small. The audience was having a ball, and we were in guitar heaven.

ADAM FAITH was very much part of my initiation to pop music. He was distinguished from the rest by his unmistakable lisped pronunciation of 'baby', as, 'boi-beh', in his hit song, 'What Do You Want' (if you don't want money), and epitomised the divide between the older generation's idea of a vocalist and that of us teenagers. My personal favourite Faith song was a B side called, 'Big Time'. To me, in ninety fifty nine, 'Big Time' was one of those songs that if you really like it, one learns all the words and bores everyone for hours. 'Big Time' said what we wanted to be. Faith was blonde and suave, and good material and style for Dean Fane; so, without hesitation, The Sandstorms brushed up on some of Adam's stuff and we put it in the gig list. Some of his songs included strong orchestral accompaniment and studio effect production, but none-the-less, we managed to present acceptable versions.

THE SEARCHERS MADE THEIR OWN STYLISED IMPRESSION
on the craft of popular music. Playing The Searchers original, fascinating rhythmic creations gave The Sandstorms a lift. 'Sweets for My Sweet', 'Sugar and Spice' and 'Needles and Pins' although prickly, were happy feelers. They had a distinctive musical patter which is difficult to put down in writing but I'll experiment. Their sound went something like this: sing, "Dum, diddle, diddle, diddle, dum, diddle, diddle, diddle, dum, diddle, diddle, diddle, dum." Now do it again, and at the same time, simultaneously at once, sing, 'Sweets for my Sweet', etc, etc, over the "Dum, diddle, diddle, diddle" part. Perhaps try it with another person doing the "Dum, diddle, diddle" bit. Where is all this going?

DUTY, COURAGE AND STOICISM OF INDIVIDUAL SANDSTORMS
above and beyond their own personal safety was applied on more than one occasion, and here are two prime examples. Tony developed pneumonia and became seriously ill. Overriding all the advice of his doctor and

mother, he dragged himself out of bed, went downstairs to the phone and insisted to Charlie that we pick him up for that night's booking. It was in Winchester, so a forty mile drive. Needless to say, his devotion to the band was so strong that even with a burning fever, but feeling cold and totally wretched (my Mother gave him a hot water bottle and covered him with a blanket for the journey in the car), he soldiered on and did the gig, never missing a note, singing-n-playing as well as ever; his croaky voice was brilliant for the Blues. Engrossed, as the audience were in their enjoyment of the rocking sounds of The Sandstorms, they were completely oblivious to the pre-show scenario that had taken place in the wings. Dave, Charlie, Eddie, and I had been privy to the spectacle of Tony, in his perspiring distressed state, on the verge of physical collapse, dosing up with strong painkillers.

A SECOND DEED OF PURE HEROISM was exercised by me whilst at work. A huge bowl of bubbling, boiling water was spilt over me, causing a serious accident. The scalding hot liquid poured down my legs, below the knees, penetrating my shoes-n-socks. Feet steaming, I was rolling on the floor in a state of shock and pain, whilst my friends administered some rather inept (smearing the burns with butter), but appreciated, first aid. Eventually, an ambulance, with its bell ringing, rushed me to Boscombe Hospital. Extra agony had to be endured as the nurse, obviously enjoying her work, surgically removed the blistered strips and remnants of my wasted flesh. By the time my Father came to drive me home from the hospital, the conscientious nurse had wrapped my red raw, skinless feet in layers of gauze wadding, swathed them in yards of cream-coloured, stretchy crepe bandages, and finally secured the two bundles with a giant safety pin. Back home, my only respite was to retire to bed, and there, elevate my throbbing limbs. Therein lies the rub, because that very same evening, The Sandstorms had, not one, but ironically, two gigs to honour. We were supposed to play an early spot at The Pavilion prior to a visiting well-known band (The Moody Blues, I think), then break down our kit and rush off to The Star Inn, Ringwood, for a blazing shindig. From my casualty position, prostrate on the bed, pillows for leg elevation to stem the searing pain, parents running errands to-n-fro at my every whinging whim, I was feeling waves-n-pangs of ambivalence as to whether or not I would be able to fulfil the band's commitments. My doubts were not all pain related; my cool, swaggering Fonz-like image had also been severely demeaned, and I wasn't relishing the idea of standing on stage, looking like a half-dressed zombie. In the end, pride, commitment, and that good old doctor entertainment took over and the gigs were done.

Sadly, and with much regret, I have to acknowledge the fact that despite the gallant-n-brave conduct displayed by these two stalwarts of rock-n-roll, no medals or citations were nominated or awarded.

The Sandstorms, Starlight Club, Tuckton

THE SANDSTORMS ALMOST WITH THE BEATLES is a sad

recollection. During The Beatles' week's performance at The Gaumont, Bournemouth, it was arranged that several groups, including The Sandstorms, would perform in a marquee erected near the beach, at The Pier Approach. All the bands were gathered, and played to the excited throng of fans who awaited the arrival of their heroes. The Beatles had been scheduled to sign autographs in the band marquee, on a six foot trestle table, complete with four gold chairs, paper-n-pens. The time came-n-went, and everybody's disappointment was confirmed when a hot, embarrassed representative came down after speaking to The Beatles, to announce that they'd had to leave in order to get to their next gig ..... and as Stanley Unwin would have said, "Deep sorrow!"

MY FIRST FLIRTATION WITH THE REMARKABLE CHUCK BERRY'S MUSIC AND LYRICS was at a gig in the Downstairs Club and

had a profound effect on our repertoire and style. Whilst packing up my gear (still wearing my lens free Hank Marvin type glasses), a black guy sauntered over to me and said, "Hey man, if you had white shoes and threw the shades, you'd be as good as Chuck Berry." He disappeared, and out of naivety I asked Dave, "Who's Chuck Berry?" "He's some guy who plays guitar," Dave informed, "And sings at the same time." Next day I had bought my first Berry record, and I was on the road to forty odd years of enjoying his music. It would be true to say that Chuck Berry had a profound effect on my guitar playing, and therefore, for Chuck's eightieth birthday, we produced the Corkscrew Play Chuck Berry album which, I'm proud to say, is featured on his personal website. Corkscrew Band (Roger, Sandra and Dick) also produced a Chuck Berry eightieth birthday bash at the Allendale Centre in Wimborne, Dorset. I can also claim to have played alongside the great man, and was renowned, by friends, audiences and Army mates, for my interpretation of his famous 'Duck Walk'.

I once waited excitedly outside the stage door at the back of the Winter Gardens, and Chuck, disappointingly, as he was the master of songs with Mustang Fords and Cadillacs motovating in the lyrics, arrived in a beaten up, rusty old Ford Consul – anticlimax! We used to play sets at The Queens Garden Restaurant at the Lansdowne which was run by this fun Chinese chap called Robert who played guitar, and most nights, with very little encouragement, would get up and do a convincing, pelvic thrusting Elvis impression (but without the weight and white rhinestone suit which came later). It was a big open plan restaurant with a small, circular parquet blocked dance floor and slightly raised stage, all sophisticatedly draped at the back in heavy red velvet curtains. Stereotypical Chinese flocked wallpaper decor created a warm ambience, including the customary gold-n-red dragons and pagodas, and the diners were bathed in salubrious oriental piped music. Robert and I were both good mates. I was a regular customer and we had a laugh over scrumptious food in his restaurant, like chop suey and sweet-n-sour pork balls. Another thing, both of us shared the same discerning taste in girls, suits and cars. Smiling his broad infectious smile, menu tucked under his arm, Robert would stroll over to the dining table, and having pre-empted my taste, would conjure up my favourite tipple, 'Nuits St. Georges'. Adopting an overemphasised, obsequious theatrical stoop, but with tongue firmly in cheek, he would often compliment me on my company, and my choice of new suit, if I was wearing one. Our suits were flashy, well cut, tight fitting, double breasted three piece products from a tailor trading under the name of 'Take Six' on the King's Road, London. Conspiratorially, he used to discreetly hinge his suit jacket open to one side, revealing the label sewn to the inside pocket, and, as 'though we were members of a secret fraternity, I would comply by doing the same. Once it was established that we were both carrying the same identification, 'Take Six labels', we responded childishly like two secret agents by swiftly closing them.

Chuck Berry was playing at the bowling alley (over which, on top of the multi-storey car park, was The Outlook Club owned by Jimmy Saville), and the joint was rolling and swarming with young, hyped-up bubbling people. Robert used to invite the bands to his restaurant after gigs, and he told me that Chuck was coming in later. Having noticed Robert go back stage with Chuck as soon as the concert was over, I wasted no time, and was out of the auditorium, up the multi-storey car park, and into my hot rod, Ford Squire station wagon. You know, the model with the wooden moulding along the sides, and the back seats that would drop down into a nice comfy bed. No guessing how my mind worked when I first saw that feature. Squealing the tyres, James Bond fashion, I hurtled my passion wagon down the helter-skelter multi-storey levels of concrete, out into the street, up through the three gears, and at a top speed of an almost heart stopping fifty miles an hour, I blazed up the Old Christchurch Road to The Queens Garden Chinese Restaurant. As promised, and on cue, Chuck came in with his entourage, but didn't eat or drink anything, just sat smiling his enigmatic cheeky smile. Apparently, he wasn't drinking as he was driving, because he didn't trust anyone else at the wheel. After acquiring his autograph on a menu, he let me keep the pencil that he had signed it with, and for years and years I treasured it, until eventually, sadly, I lost it through over sharpening. Co-incidentally, we just happened to have our kit there on stage so, devilishly, I asked him if he would sit in and jam with us. It was all a bit of a set up, but he was happy to join us on the condition that I play the lead parts and he'd do the rhythm. I wanted to do Johnny B Goode, but he didn't, so we did 'Wee, Wee Hours' as it was getting late. Then, just as we finished, determined to make the most of the moment, I played the intro to Johnny B Goode and he gave me this look. Then all of a sudden, he started up with that chugging rhythm, and there I was playing lead guitar on Johnny B Goode with Chuck Berry. The ultimate exhilarating experience, never to be repeated, indelibly etched in my brain cells for life.

THE DAVE CLARK FIVE were innovative and fun, and probably the second main band involved in the British music invasion of the U.S.A. Eye-catching and smartly attired in uniform blazers with white flannels, Dave Clark's crew projected an up-tempo, jolly stage persona, and they managed, in nineteen sixty four, to knock their eminence, The Beatles, off the top spot of what was then known cosily as the 'Hit Parade' with their creative, repetitive drum thumping beat number, 'Glad All Over'. I would say that the charts were more varied and healthier back then, with every genre of music, happily jostling with each other – Ballads, Rock, Jazz, Folk, Orchestral, and even Comedy. The clean, wholesome, parent, and Archbishop-in-cloisters friendly image of The Dave Clark Five got them onto the American Ed Sullivan Show, no less than eighteen times. Dave and his Five was another conformist rattling dimension brought to the ever widening scope of the sixties music scene. Our drummer Dave, with the gusto of Dusty Springfield, but without the black eye shadow, thrashed out the Dave Clark sound on his tight skins with great delight.

It's difficult for people not around then to realise that pop music in the media was scarce in those days. There was a programme on the television called **JUKE BOX JURY**, with a host called David Jacobs, and a panel of scrutineers who would listen to a selection of new releases and predict their success by holding up pieces of cardboard saying 'Hit' or 'Miss'. However, pop music stations on the wireless hadn't been thought of, and, to kids who, like secret agents in the French Resistance, clandestinely tuned into Radio Luxembourg on their transistors, it never seemed a possibility, and if DJ's were caught, they would get years of hard labour on a treadmill! Every sixties composition didn't just begin to exist, like magic at the beginning of the decade. It was gradually created, and then fed, tune by song, into the popular music repertoire. If now, we attend a sixties theme night disco, or party, the whole shooting match of sixties' material would be there on tap. But in nineteen sixty, there was very little. It wasn't until all the new bands began to immerge and start writing that a serious portfolio got under way. At the beginning, when The Sandstorms were playing instrumentals and songs by Elvis Presley, Buddy Holly, Tommy Steele and Cliff Richard, the likes of The Beatles, The Rolling Stones, The Merseybeats, Gerry and The Pacemakers, and Billy J Kramer and The Dakotas, etc, were still unheard of, and in fact, some hadn't even been formed. When I first asked the assistant in Brights' record shop to order me a Beatles song, she took a while finding out who they were, and to tell the truth, I wasn't quite sure either. Eventually, after a week or so, I went in to collect it and was most disappointed. I can't remember what I thought it was going to be. Perhaps, 'Please, Please Me', but it turned out to be, Tony Sheridan and The Beatles, with 'My Bonnie' (lies over the ocean), and on the flipside, 'When The Saints Go Marching In'. Most of the Mersey bands, including The Beatles, started

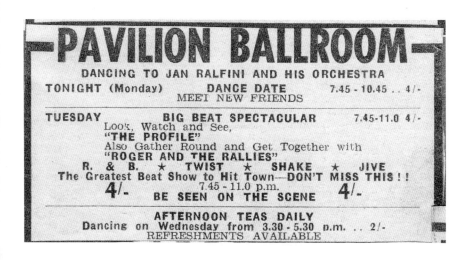

Roger and The Rallies, Pavilion

off playing skiffle and all the well known, traditional standards that were featured by hotel dance bands and trad jazz classics. I also bought Tony Sheridan and The Beatles playing, 'Sweet Georgia Brown'. Basically, until everyone followed The Beatles lead and began to pen their own stuff, rock groups were playing American 'rocked up' versions of the classic dance band material.

THE DELECTABLE MISS WORLD, ANN SYDNEY, was born in Poole, Dorset, and for twelve months, she managed to sprinkle some fairy dust sparkle over the place. She was obviously glamorous, well-spoken and projected a reasonably educated persona, whereas a few of the winners came over, rightly or wrongly, as slightly dimmer. I can't remember if she wanted to raise children, ride horses, and bring about world peace, but it's highly likely, and would be have been compulsory for a Miss World. During her 'reigning year', she was always rushing around opening something in her official capacity, or attending functions, sometimes with us in The Pavilion Ballroom. It wasn't uncommon to see her around town, and I clearly remember occupying the same lift as her in Bobby's apartment store, by The Square. I'm sure that she got out at lingerie, or was that my overactive imagination? The lifts in Bobby's and Beales' apartment stores used to have an attendant onboard. The liveried attendant (sometimes with jangling war medals proudly displayed and an obligatory limp) would operate the lift (pressing the appropriate buttons), and announce the various floor numbers, accompanied by their relevant wares. "Going up," the attendant would declare. "First floor haberdashery, second floor furniture." Then, returning us all to terrafirma, "Going down, ladies underwear..." It used to amuse us for hours.

BEING IN A SIXTIES ROCK GROUP gave us a unique, privileged insight into the glamorous world of entertainment, and set us apart from the mundane routine of normal, drab daily life. Being a member of a group added another dimension to our period as teenagers. We became, in a petite local form, a commodity of the era, a reference point for those who attended our gigs, and perhaps met, fell in love, married and had children, and all as a consequence of our gig. Perhaps we were playing, 'their tune'. Personally, as a musician, although I looked forward to going to a dance, I didn't go for the dancing per se. Rather, I loved watching bands for a practical reason. Our days were spent working on becoming the reason why people went to a dance, a club, a ballroom, a venue. We wanted to be the centre of their motivation, the name on the bill, displayed in the newspaper ad, the name on the poster outside The Pavilion, The Winter Gardens, The Royal Ballrooms, the name scrawled in chalk on the blackboard outside the local pub, the name in ink on the flyer and on the ticket stub. There was a key, an instrument that would fulfil our burning ambitions, the catalyst that would propel us to the centre of attention and make us the reason for the audience turning up each night, which was the guitar. For some, it was the drums, or the vocal ability. Unlike most teenagers, we frequented a different wavelength, a parallel world on the margins of regular life, a private place that the rest of Joe Public could never visit – another dimension. This spiritual place harbours the lonely, grafting, devoted life that is the truth behind the lights, the greasepaint and the applause. We looked at the careers of our idols in a clinical, scrutinising way. We didn't just listen sheepishly to the music of the times. We had to analyse it, we needed to know the key they were playing it in, the method they used to play a memorable, impressive guitar solo, the equipment they were using to create the distinctive sounds being produced, what they were wearing, and where we could buy the same boots to emulate and reproduce the visually pleasing aesthetics for our punters. In many respects, our lives were insular. Many solitary hours were spent slavishly working on our instruments. We imprisoned ourselves in our backrooms, honing in our craft, that we might be admired for our dexterity and skill and ability to reproduce the sounds-n-songs that pleased our audiences. Whatever the heartache, whatever frustration or disappointment that raked us, in the end, it was all worth it. It supplied us with priceless, unrepeatable memories, and nourishing, life-giving food for thought, and they are all lovingly stored and cherished.

FREDDIE AND THE DREAMERS stage act was thrilling to emulate. Freddie's prancing and jumping around gave us a good excuse (not that we needed one) to spring all over the stage like demented frogs. Again, they were a sign of the times with energising songs-n-music with a positive message, not like the Blues with all that negativity and 'baby's leaving me when I get up in the morning' misery. That's why we enjoyed the likes of Chuck Berry; he was fun, singing about girls-n-cars and frivolous trivia. And what happened to all the comedy bands and songs that used to be popular and even in the charts, like 'Right Said Fred' by Bernard Cribbens, and even the thespian send-up by Peter Sellers of The Beatles' 'Hard Day's Night'?

To maximise on the many available venues in and around town, and in order to exploit our insatiable desire to play, we came up with a pulchritudinous plan. The Sandstorms, duplicitously, decided to work in tandem with themselves (what?), and so, during the latter stages of their brief but vital existence, they also traded as a (successful as it turned out) band called, **THE DYNOSONIC JERKS**. Doing so, whatever the ethical argument, gave us the advantage of being able to indulge in two styles of music. As The Dynosonic Jerks, we concentrated on

R&B, whereas, The Sandstorms were spread more evenly across the spectrum of popular music. This situation meant that The Dynsonic Jerks, although leaning heavily towards R&B, possessed the ability and the repertoire to be flexible, as was necessary, to meet the public's musical demands. Ultimately, and from a lucrative point of view, it meant double the amount of bookings, and double the amount of money. Not being household names, a simple change of stage costume (smart suits and ties for The Sandstorms, and slovenly waistcoat gear for The Dynosonic Jerks) was enough to disguise us, and present the image of two different bands. The dancers got on happily with their dancing, the management were happy, and we provided the happy music. Result ..... everybody was happy.

THE CLIFF RICHARD AND THE SHADOWS 50TH ANNIVERSARY CONCERT AT the NIA hall in Birmingham was absolutely massive and contained thousands of vibrant fans. From our seats, two thirds of the way back, halfway up one side of the ginormous cavern, I scanned the neat rows of people packed in colourful quadrangles, looking like legions of Roman battle groups. The seating rose so high, it seemed as though they were stuck to the walls, and reminded me of a crowd scene in a painting, where if examined too closely, the illusion is revealed, and all the faces are just hundreds of pinkie-white paint brush blobs. The whole event was like being in a time-capsule, except that a leak had been sustained, and all the inmates had actually aged simultaneously. We were all the mature children of a certain generation, the late fifties, early sixties. Even-so, our idols, like us, had also endured the past fifty years, but for some reason – perhaps because they had lived a rich, pampered and stress-free life on the profits of record sales to us – remarkably, they still looked exactly the same. There was tall willowy Hank, with his trade mark horn-rimmed glasses. Bruce was still strumming rhythm guitar with his usual toothy (they looked a bit white!), cheery grin. The bass player was new (there have been many replacements over the years since the original Jet Harris left), middle-aged, but still had all his faculties and could move, just like his predecessors. Brian clattered energetically on the drums. Not only that, they still had complete heads of hair. Bruce and the bass player were grey, but it was hair and it was their own, and there was a vital spring in their stride as they stepped out that choreographic piece of history, a must-see at all Shadows concerts, the legendary, one-n-only, "Shadows' Walk". The common bond I felt within the congregation was tangible. Everyone was relaxed, at one with life, and it was wonderfully reassuring to know that there were millions of gentle, like-minded and civilised people, all joined in celebration of this happy, heart-warming and inoffensive music. Cliff Richard and The Shadows' music offered us hope and promise; it had endured the rigours of time, and is of such a calibre, that after all these years, it brought us all back together again. Whilst a large majority of the

audience was gasping for oxygen, just negotiating the few steps to their seats, Cliff, being his usual athletic self, literally bounded onto the stage, and proceeded to sing and prance from one side of the enormous stage to the other for almost the entire evening. Between numbers, however much he'd run around, he never appeared to falter for breath when speaking. They never neglected our desire, and played all the favourites from our formative years. The culmination naturally being 'F.B.I.', 'Move It' ("The best rock-n-roll song," John Lennon) and finally, to a standing ovation, and as Cliff orated so movingly, the one thing everyone in that auditorium would always be, the original, 'Young Ones!'

BY NINETEEN SIXTY FOUR, a fifteen year old girl singer, Lulu, and her band, **The Luvvers** were 'shouting' the beginning of their career, whereas in contrast, The Sandstorms, and their twin group, The Dynosonic Jerks, had by then fallen silent. Guitars were relegated to their cases, amps-n-drums put into mothballs, and as young, life challenging and expectant young men, we set off to experience whatever the world had to throw at us. A never to be forgotten, never to be repeated experience was finished.

WHAT HAPPENED TO THE SANDSTORMS AND DOES ANY ONE CARE? because inevitably, as with 'Old Man River', life flows on, and

The Sandstorms, sucked into that whirling hypothetical current of time, somehow swept majestically into the future, and with the advent of the internet and cyber space, eventually dissolved and reformed as, The Virtual Sandstorms. Roger lived his dream of becoming a soldier in 1964 when he went off (against the will of his parents and friends) to Winchester, and enlisted with The Green Jackets. The Green Jackets marched very fast, and had a tough military record and proud reputation. Their gallant-n-fearless background was brilliantly conveyed by the author, Bernard Cornwall, in his exciting and dramatic books and TV series, 'Sharpe'. Having got some time in, Roger became professionally involved in the entertainment industry as an actor and cabaret artiste. Later still, with his wife Sandra (keyboards and caller), they created Corkscrew Barn Dance Band. Dave went on to became an engineer, toolmaker, and later, a property developer and landlord (not of a pub), and well respected, hard working pillar of the community. Tony, I think, worked for an oil company in London. He was an amazing bloke, could play guitar and sing second to none. Mike left The Sandstorms after a Royal Ballrooms gig, and went to sea with the Royal Navy, a family tradition. He was also an impressive photographer. He later went on to other things, but I'm not sure what, but I know he done well, and as far as I know, always respected his religious beliefs. Dean, I'm sure never touched another pork pie, but did pursue various successful business projects, including a fund-raising company, and at one time owned a real good, busy, hot-n-steamy cafe. (Sorry – caff!) He remained a lifelong Cliff Richard fan. Joss left hotfoot after the Moose Hall punch-up and was never seen again. Perhaps he became a Trappist monk, or reclused himself, singing lonesome laments on the back of his faithful ol' horse, as a solitary sheep drover in far outback Oz. Nobody knows. We can only speculate. Eddie joined the Military Police and the Fire Brigade, thus reflecting his arresting personality and burning ambition. Dave Woodbury (keys) became a local entertainment agent, and drove a fleet of electric, ecological, cars. John (keys) went to America where he worked as a rocket scientist at Cape Canaveral. His career rocketed to great heights.

Roger now

THE BEATLES' EFFECT

The depth-n-breadth of their music style and diversity in composition and their massive effect and influence on the culture of music, psychology and fashion worldwide, was absolutely magnificent. They began as a skiffle group, then moved on to be the crisp, smart suited, Cuban-heeled cheeky Liverpool 'Fab Four', and morphed from the four mop heads into the long haired, bearded, psychedelic Sergeant Pepper, garish, military uniformed clad, spiritual cloud 9ers. Their influence on just about everything, everywhere, was phenomenal. They were musical prophets.

THE ROLLING STONES' PLACE IN THE HISTORY OF ROCK

They began as a 'Chuck Berry' covers' band, and one of the best (apart from the unsurpassable anthem to the great musician, 'Corkscrew Play Chuck Berry') but after falling out of love with their idol (familiarity breeds contempt), they went on (with some external pushing) to compose and create their own inimitable style of rhythm-n-bluesy, rock-n-rolly, gritty music. Together, with their high profile persona of hard drinking, peacock strutting stage performance (even as pensioners), they have become a major element on the current world music stage. Their first hit was 'Come On' and the second was a Beatles' tune, 'I Wanna Be Your Man'.

In contrast, The Rolling Stones have become wizened, but great 'Pension Rockers' in a groovy-groove, whereas, The Beatles, in their inimitability, remain encapsulated in time (John, was he a prophet? was shot, and George died), and therefore remain, forever young.

AND OF COURSE CHUCK BERRY is a legendary icon of popular music,

a most enriching, influential guitarist, poetic lyricist, and the undisputed Father of Rock-n-Roll. A dynamic performer, the consummate entertainer and an inspiration to many guitarists, Chuck Berry has been an integral element for popular music, and thus will remain in the realms of music folklore. No other artist within the rock-n-roll genre has been so crucial in its development as Chuck Berry. He moulded the rock guitar's voice forever, and without him, there would be no Beatles, Rolling Stones, Beach Boys, and many others of that ilk. He created the definitive rock-n-roll guitar intro with 'Johnny B Goode'. I warrant that every guitarist on the globe has had a bash at that lick. He catapulted the distinctive chunky-chunky rockabilly rhythm into the mainstream where it is now the standard 4/4 rock-n-roll beats. He set the artistic standard of rock lyrics, and to quote Brian Wilson, "Chuck Berry wrote all the greatest songs, and came up with all the rock-n-roll beats. Those who do not claim him as the seminal influence, or profess a liking to his music and showmanship, show their ignorance of rock's development, as well as his place as rock music's first great creator. Elvis may have fuelled rock-n-roll's imagery, but Chuck Berry was its heartbeat and original mindset."

As a tribute to the master, Chuck Berry, I produced a CD, **Corkscrew Play Chuck Berry**, available online, or at www.corkscrewband.co.uk

Those fleeting teenage days of innocence, filled with vigour, hope and joy.

That brief happy margin before the bitter truth of life.

ROGER DOWNTON

THE END

OF THE SANDSTORMS AND THE DYNOSONIC JERKS
WELL SPENT ROCK-N-ROLL YOUTH AND POP AS WE KNEW IT